S0-AXQ-741

In dedication to my grandfather,
Henry Eugene Littlefield 1903-1989

Pup,

Without your ever-present twinkling humor, your razor-sharp wit, and your incredible stories that I loved so very much as a child and young adult, I know I would have neither the courage nor the ability to try my hand at storytelling about the family, the farms, and a way of life that we continue to cherish. You will always be my hero.

Acknowledgements

This book of short stories has come together over a fairly long period of time. That is to say, I have been writing stories about my family and the farms we owned and operated, for over 25 years. It started out innocently enough, I really just wanted to preserve some of the family memories, stories told to me by my elders, some of the funny moments that continually replay in movie-like form in my mind, and my thoughts on growing up in this family, on those farms.

This was a very private affair initially. I never realized how much my family supported these stories until I started bugging them for memories. It was common at family get-togethers to spend much of that time reminiscing among ourselves and listening to my elders tell stories and yarns of years gone by...something that has always fascinated me, and the primary motivation to write these stories. Also, I didn't think anyone else would be interested in my stories. I have never had any formal training or education in being a writer, I wasn't sure the stories were good enough, or interesting enough to share. I've come to realize this may be a very common affliction among people who write stories of a personal nature for public consumption.

So, PLEASE, like my stories. Just kidding...sorta.

Once I started letting family and friends read these stories, the feedback was very positive.

They loved the stories, as they were invested in them. They also said the stories were well written and very descriptive. They encouraged me to write, write, write. So, I did, did, did.

And, I began to bug them continuously about their memories of this family and the farms. I would call various family members at all hours to ask for a point of reference or clarification, or for their memories of one event or another. I became something of a pest. Not one of my family members ever denied me time to talk about the story I was writing, willingly offered their memories, and helped with points of clarification. I could not have made this happen without them. This endeavor truly became a family project. I hope you like our stories, and you know I can't express my appreciation enough for all your support, encouragement, and help. You are amazing!

My immediate family has endured this obsession of mine for many years, too. They have been rocks, each and every one. I'm a lucky man. Thank you, guys.

Patricia Newell of North Country Press, and her staff, have been so instrumental in helping this project through the editing and publishing phase. Pat's nurturing demeanor and her patience cannot be appreciated enough. A special thanks to fellow author and friend John Ford, Sr. John, without your helpful suggestions, I may have never met Pat. Thank you.

To my daughter-in-law, Allison Harrell, I am incredibly pleased that you would use your artistic talents to design this book cover. It makes this whole project that much more special.

To the memories of our beloved grandparents, Henry & Selena Littlefield, and our uncle and aunt, Gene & Wilda Littlefield: You defined this family. Not a day goes by that this family doesn't think about each of you. Your memories will live on forever. I am honored and privileged to tell these stories about our incredible family.

Prologue

The Farm

Many things have changed since my boyhood on the farm. To start with, there is no more farm where my grandparents lived.

No more house even.

The house and cattle barn were razed some years back, the chicken barn was torn down a few years prior to that. The old outbuildings have all fallen in and rotted away. The pastures have all gone to seed and have become part of the surrounding woods. Where the old chicken barn used to sit is now my Uncle Stub's sawmill, and his granddaughter lives in a mobile home where my grandparents' farmhouse used to sit.

The little house that my Uncle Gene and his family lived in when I was really young is gone. In fact, the house was moved across the road to a neighbor's lot and it now is used as a barn.

In its place sits a greenhouse that my cousin operates and sells plants and flowers from. Where the cattle barn sat is now just an empty space, and beyond that, where my Uncle Stub and his family lived in a mobile home (which at one time was pasture) is now just an empty lot. The old farm pond is now nothing more than a mud puddle. My father's house still remains—it is still across the road from the old farm. My nephew now resides there. My father now lives in Florida.

There really is nothing left of the original farm but memories. It is those memories that have inspired me to write these stories—my way of preserving the love of a way of life, of a farm family that centered around Henry and Selena Littlefield, and their six children.

i

Both of my grandparents have now passed on, but there is not a single day in the lives of their children and grandchildren that they are not remembered and thought of. They were both so very instrumental in what defines each of us, that it is impossible for each of us to not consider our memories, and ask ourselves, "What would Pup do in this situation?" or, "How did Mamie manage that?"

Henry and Selena Littlefield, (affectionately dubbed "Pup" and "Mamie" by their grandchildren, "Father and Mother" to their children) were married on September 21, 1924, and had six children. The first child, Marion, died shortly after childbirth, but the other five kids grew up as part of the farm family. The oldest, my Uncle Gene, born in 1927, and then my Dad, Warren, born in 1931, followed by my Uncle Mo, born 1934, then Aunt Bev seven years later, with Unc Gary (Stub) being the "baby", born four years later in 1945.

As of today, the family has branched out to include 10 grandchildren, 22 great-grandchildren, and many great-great-grandchildren. It's hard to keep up.

Today, farming is a dying, if not dead, lifestyle here in Maine. One cannot survive trying to farm any longer. The poultry plants have all closed and moved south, so the one-time income stream from raising chickens is gone. The price of grain, baling twine, medicine and vaccinations for the animals, fencing, barn and building maintenance, tractors and farm equipment, and associated repairs have all skyrocketed out of sight. Sadly, the cost of maintaining a working farm far exceeds the amount of money one can expect to receive in return.

This is why none of Henry and Selena's family farms anymore, except Uncle Gene's son and grandson. My cousin Gene still operates and lives on the "Other Farm", which I will describe later. Cousin Gene also works a full-time job off the farm. (Ironically at the same chemical manufacturing plant my father worked at many years ago.) So does his son Lyle. This family all works full-time jobs off the farm so they can support the farm that the entire family grew up on. The very farm that has had so much influence on each of us. The very farm where a lot of the memories and the stories that I am writing come from. This farm is located on the most beautiful land in Waldo County, and I'm sure it has a monetary value that far exceeds more money than my cousin has ever seen or expects to ever see. Yet, he has made the commitment to not let a way of life that we all cherished die.

I'm not sure I can express the amount of gratitude and respect I have for him and his family's resolve to maintain a way of life the entire family loves so very much. I am in awe of their work ethic. Holding down full-time jobs off the farm while also doing the work of maintaining a farm, and the resolute conviction to not buckle under and take the "easy" way out. I know that Mamie and Pup, wherever they may be, are smiling at him and are resting comfortably. It is cousin Gene's sort of resolve that is dying in this country, as fast as the farming family is.

When I grew up on the family farm in the 60s and early 70s our family operated three separate farms. First there was Mamie and Pup's, my grandparents' farm, which was also considered the homestead. There was little question that Pup and Mamie were the patriarch/matriarch of our family. Everything began and ended with them. They set all the standards and most every family affair was held at their farm and in their farmhouse. Secondly, there was Uncle Gene's farm, and last, but surely not least, there is the "Other Farm". The Other Farm, has always been a magical place to me and is featured prominently in my stories.

Pup and Mamie's farm featured a classic white New England three-bedroom, story-and-a-half farmhouse with an attached shed, and an unattached big red barn that housed the milk cows, a bull or two at times, the occasional goat, pigs, laying hens and even a pet crow or two, in the tie-up. The tie-up was the part of the barn where the animals were housed and had two doors. A smaller one which was used to access the area, and a larger one where the animals would be let into and out of the pasture, and to wheelbarrow out the animal waste to dump in an ever-growing pile behind the barn. The manure was then used at different times to fertilize the hay fields and the gardens. In the main and larger part of the barn there was a two-story haymow. The door to the haymow was one large 20' x 15' door, painted white, which slid open and shut on a rail at the top. There were a couple of out buildings and sheds which housed farming equipment, or animals if the tie up happened to be full. There was a large three-story Quonset-style chicken house which measured 100' long by 50' wide, with a two-story grain room/coal room attached. This building housed, when filled to capacity, about 20,000 chickens.

Surrounding the buildings were about 100 acres of pasture/woods which featured lots of woods roads, old apple trees, a farm pond or two, and our property line bordered on a working gravel pit owned by my grandfather's brother. I can assure you, having a 100-acre gravel/sand pit in your backyard is the uber sandbox to play in, along with acres upon acres of woodland, creeks, ponds and old woods roads to explore and exercise your childhood fantasies on, be it playing cowboys and Indians, or Army, or even skating on the ponds in the winter with a large bonfire on the shore, sliding down the huge hills in the pit, playing hide and seek, or many other outdoor games I loved and enjoyed as a kid.

There was a time when this was the only farm in the family. Unc Gene and his wife, Aunt Wilda lived in a little house on the other side of the driveway from Mamie's and Pup's, Dad and Mom lived just down and across the road in a little house, and Unc Stub and his wife, Aunt Brenda, lived just to the west side of the farmhouse in a mobile home, which used to be part of the pasture, across from Dad and Mom's house, in what most old timers might refer to as "the dell". Unc Mo had gone off to college, got himself educated, and was living in Virginia, along with his beautiful bride, my Aunt Julia, (a true southern belle from Virginia) and was busy pursuing his career in education at Old Dominion University. My Aunt Bev was close at hand, she and her husband, Uncle Roy, were busy building their family in nearby Searsmont, Maine.

Then, in the early 50s my grandfather and Unc Gene bought a 200-acre parcel of land which was dubbed "The Other Farm". Oh my! There may not be a more beautiful piece of land in all of Waldo County than the Other Farm. From the driveway going into the big two-story Quonset 75' by 35' barn, one faces the south and can overlook the many acres of beautiful fields dotted with the fluorescent yellow of dandelions, the soft amber of the growing timothy that would soon be hay, the deep rich green of the grass, the purples of the clover which contrast with the snow white puffs of the sheep, the black and white surreal pattern of the Holstein cows, and the sleek dark shimmering coats of the horses, all punctuated by the deep blue sky with its white and brown specks of seagulls and hawks floating lazily round and round. These fields slope downhill to a semi-wooded valley that has a dogwood- and alder-lined stream babbling through it and is excellent for trout fishing. From there the forest becomes dense with maple, beech, white and gray birch, oak, hemlock, pine, spruce, and ash and the land begins a rapid upward climb that peaks at the southern-most property line. In the autumn this forest offers a kaleidoscope of iridescent colors from the turning leaves of the hardwoods, offset by the rich forest green of the evergreen softwoods. This is the second highest hill in Waldo County, I'm told, and it does offer an incredible visual landscape. Even in the winter months the view overlooking The Other Farm is breathtaking with its blanket of stark white waves of pristine snow and ice glittering in the brisk sun highlighted with those beautiful evergreens and the ice cold cobalt blue of the skies. As I mentioned earlier, this place is magical. The "Shangri-La" of farms.

The Other Farm also has a bubbling spring that produces very cold and clean water, which came in handy during the summer months when we were haying, shearing the sheep, or spreading manure on the fields. A nice little pit stop where we would take a breather and be refreshed by drinking from the old tin cup which hung from a branch beside the spring. It has a farm pond about 100 yards from the barn which we kids would skinny-dip in to wash the hay chaff and sweat from ourselves after stacking the bales of hay in the mow. In the forest I described, we would cut wood, timber for sale for pilings, pulpwood to be sold to the paper mills, and of course firewood, both for the family and for sale. We would tend the sheep, a flock of over 400 head, shear the wool in June to be sold to the woolen mills, and the lambs would be sold in the fall to the markets for meat. The cattle were for the milk and meat for the family, and some for sale as well. The horses were mostly for pleasure riding, but there were also work horses and mules that were used to pull scoots or wagons loaded with wood.

There seemed to always be a various assortment of other animals/birds as well, ranging from turkeys, geese and ducks, to goats, and even an old donkey named "Ed Muskie" after Maine's well-known political son.

In 1960, Unc Gene bought another farm, one that abutted "The Other Farm". His family's new home featured a two-and-a-half story farmhouse with attached shed to which a very large four-story 60' x 40' barn was attached. It also had a smaller 35' x 25' barn that was unattached at the western edge of the property with its own tie-up, and behind the farmhouse a large three-story 60' x 35' Quonset barn on the northern edge of the property.

This farm has over 150 acres of mostly fields and pasture. The four-story barn that was attached to the house by means of the shed was actually moved there by a team of oxen from a farm up on Cross Pond some five miles away some time long before Unc bought the place. I always marveled at how such a large building could be moved by what today would be considered primitive means. Both the Quonset barn out back and the large barn attached to the farmhouse via the shed, were used to raise chickens. Between the two barns another 20,000 birds were raised on top of the 20,000 in the chicken house at Pup's farm.

Back in the 1940s through the 1970s, Belfast, Maine, was known as the "chicken capital of the world". There were two large chicken processing plants in town, where over 250,000 chickens were processed daily. Most every farmer in Waldo County got in on the action and raised chickens for the owners of these two processing plants. Raising chickens was a perfect way to augment your income if you were a farmer because while the chickens required daily attention, they could be attended to in 1- to 2-hour blocks of time morning and evening, therefore leaving time to handle the many other jobs and duties that farming in Maine required. The chickens were raised in 10-week cycles, beginning with newly hatched chicks less than two days old being delivered to the freshly cleaned chicken house. The chicken house was cleaned of all the dung, feathers, dust, cobwebs, leftover grain, and water prior to the sanitation man showing up and spraying the barn from top to bottom to prevent disease. Then, the day we kids always looked forward to would happen, the day a huge truck filled with wood shavings pulled into the yard, backed up to the chicken house and proceeded to blow the entire truckload into huge piles of these shavings on each floor of the chicken house. Then the shavings were spread about four inches thick over the entire floor of each story, the stoves which were located throughout the chicken house about every 20 feet were serviced and cleaned, and then cardboard rings about 16" high were placed in a circle around each stove with an interior dimension of about 10 feet for the baby chicks to live in, near the warmth of the stove.

Spreading the shavings was always a lot of fun as a kid because it was clean, and easy to carry and spread. Bringing in the baby chicks was always a pleasure too, brand new little yellow puffs of fluffy life that peeped and scurried about. Soon the baby chicks would outgrow the cardboard circles and lose their baby appeal, and become white and gangling with almost stork-like legs. Then they would start to fill out and become mature chickens, while the air in the chicken house would become increasingly more and more stifling with a pungent ammonia smell and so thick with dust that your lungs would burn after spending the hour or so it took to fill all the feeders with grain and unclog all the self-filling watering troughs. After the 10 weeks it took to raise the birds to maturity, the processing plants would send a pick-up crew whose job was to catch and coop all the chickens and stack the filled coops onto large flatbed trucks to be hauled to the plant for processing.

Then came the most dreaded part of the process. Cleaning the chicken house. You, the reader, might be amazed at the amount of dung 20,000 chickens can produce in 10 weeks. I can tell you the floors of the chicken house were about a foot thick with the salad of shavings, dung, spilled grain and water, dust, feathers, and anything else you might imagine. I can also tell you it was usually rock hard, and required a lot of very hard backbreaking work to shovel it all out onto our old wooden bodied dump truck named "Emma". Emma was also used as a hay truck, a pulp truck, a firewood truck, etc. Don't forget the smell I described earlier. Actually, the winter months were a little easier to take as far as cleaning out the chicken house as the cold seemed to knock the smell and dust down a little, or perhaps it was because it was so cold your nose and mouth were usually numb. One did not heat the chicken house when there were no chickens within that needed to be kept warm. The cleaning out, spraying down, spreading of shavings, cleaning and servicing of stoves, setting up the cardboard rings process took about a week to ten days. Then the process would start all over again. Bring in the new chicks, raise them for 10 weeks, pickup crew coops them and hauls them off, clean out the chicken house, prepare for new chicks, repeat.

As I said, raising chickens was considered a way to augment a farmer's income. There were still many other jobs to do. I told you about the haying, which took about six weeks each summer, start to finish. I told you about shearing the sheep each June, which took just about the entire month to complete. I also mentioned spreading manure on the hay fields, which took a couple of weeks in August. I described cutting firewood, pulp wood, and timber, which was a year-round job that was done when anything else of higher priority was caught up for the moment.

There were huge gardens to plant in the spring, tend and weed throughout the summer, harvest in the early fall, and mulch and fertilize in the late fall, as these gardens not only yielded produce sold at market, but the family's food as well. This created another job, the canning, freezing, and pickling of the garden's bounty. This also included the making of the sauerkraut, which was always one of my favorite jobs. Additionally, it included the making of horseradish sauce to be jarred, an eye-watering experience. There was the slaughter, butchering, meat wrapping, and storage into the freezers throughout the family, of the beef critters, the lambs, the pigs, chickens and any game harvested through hunting, such as venison. There were always roofs that needed patching, fences that needed mending, trucks, cars, and tractors that needed servicing, farm equipment that needed repairs, a coat of paint that needed to be applied, a cellar that needed cleaning, a chimney that needed cleaning, wood that needed splitting or needed to be tiered into the woodsheds, animals that needed to be nursed by us as the mother had died, or female sheep that needed help birthing as they were breech.

There was always more to do than could be done, but it was the most fantastic way of life a boy could ever hope to have.

Somehow, in spite of all the work that was required every day on the farm, I remember spending time with my grandfather, my father, and my uncles deer hunting, rabbit hunting with our beagles, or coon hunting at night with the coon hounds. Also, ice fishing in the winter, where we would always have a fire on shore and cook hot-dogs and fillets of the fish we caught, still the best hot-dog or fish I've ever eaten, or fishing in the stream at the Other Farm in the summer, or my favorite, listening to my grandfather tell stories when he and other farmers in the neighborhood would gather on a rainy day, sometimes around Pup's hard cider barrels in his cellar. I loved to listen to those stories, I'd hang on every word and recreate the stories in my very active imagination.

His stories would range from fantastic hunting and fishing yarns, his boyhood days living on his father's farm, and how he ran away from home when he was but 14 years of age to live and work with another farmer, to his days living in Boston as a "kept man" with a nurse and visiting the blues clubs of that city in the early 1920s. Incredible adventures that kept my imagination in high gear for hours at a time.

My grandfather always seemed to have an easy and natural affinity with animals and though I never knew until just recently, his secret desire was to be a veterinarian. He seemed to be able to understand all animals, but particularly larger animals. The local vet, Dr. Whitcomb, would sometimes take my grandfather along with him to other farms where Pup seemed to have an uncanny sixth sense regarding the animal's malady and often times would offer up his own down-home remedy to give the stricken animal relief. Pup was a cow-whisperer evidently. In fact, it was while he was tending another farmer's stricken cow that he became infected with Unguium fever that nearly cost him his life.

So, I have tried to paint a colorful picture for you, the reader, as an introduction to our family and the farms we worked in my childhood. I have, hopefully, set the table, so to speak, and piqued your interest. What follows is a series of stories, all based on that farm life and of this family. Most of the stories are offered in a tongue in cheek manner, as that is how much of life was viewed by my grandparents, and you shall see the common thread of hard work, love of family and farm, and twinkling humor displayed throughout these wonderful memories. I would humbly suggest that you the reader sit back in that easy chair, relax, throw on your old flannel shirt, pour yourself a dollop of brandy, and let these stories and your imagination take you to a time gone by.

Table of Contents

Story One

Emma Gets Stripped

When I was a kid growing up in the 1960s, and then later as a teenager in the 1970s, having three farms to play on was fantastic. Across the road, in the pasture at Unc Gene's farm, buried in a pine grove near the brook, was an old one-room shack that Cuz Genie-bub and I converted into a camp, which we built onto, creating a modest two-room oasis. It featured a main room with an old potbellied wood stove in the corner, a few old ratty chairs, a scarred table and chair set, and shelves for magazines, cookware, and other assorted camp gear. The original shack became the bedroom and had two sets of bunk beds built in on each end. This camp became our hangout, a place where the adults didn't visit, and where we would congregate with our school chums for parties and general mischief.

Connecting to Unc Gene's farm was the sheep farm, known in our family as "The Other Farm".

It offered acres of fields for the sheep and cattle to graze with lots of room for horse riding and snowmobiling, the brook for fishing, and miles of tote roads in the woods for hunting and playing with the '49 Willys jeep.

However, it was Pup's farm and the surrounding land that was my playpen when I was little.

Behind the three-story chicken house was a patch of woods of about 25 acres with a tote road that led to the backfields. The ten-acre backfields were sandwiched between another 65-acre woodlot on the east, and a 100-acre commercial gravel pit and woodlot to the west. On this approximate 200 acres of playground were farm ponds for swimming, a creek to splash around in, a swamp that was a bit eerie but fun to explore, old apple orchards that still produced apples for a quick snack, a couple of long-since-used old falling down houses and out buildings for makeshift camps, a maze of old tote roads to explore and sneak about on, an old dump to dig in, and countless huge pine trees for climbing and building tree houses. That gravel pit, which was a little boy's dream come true sandbox, was a favorite place for all the neighborhood kids. The pit offered a series of gravel and sand banks, some as high as 100 feet, for climbing and sliding. In the lower section of the pit were a couple of crystal clear ponds for swimming in the summer and for ice skating in the winter. Many cold late afternoons and early evenings the neighborhood kids would congregate to ice skate and play the game of "cock the rooster" with a roaring bonfire on the edge of the pond. Many nights our parents were forced to drive to the pit and threaten us with eternal grounding if we didn't come home and do our homework and get ready for bed.

Our neighborhood consisted of approximately 30 of us kids (mostly all relatives) within an 8-10 year age difference, so the older ones looked after the younger ones. We ran the woods, fields, and the gravel pit of the neighborhood. Or at least we thought we did.

With such a large and diverse tract of land on which to play, and such a willing group of kids to play with, we developed a game called "Monster" which was part tag and part hide and go seek. The game was played over the entire neighborhood, incorporating our yards as well as the woods, fields, tote roads, and gravel pit. There was the "it" team, which typically consisted of five or six people who were responsible for finding, tagging, and then dragging the others back to "gue". Gue was a designated spot or area, typically a large tree on Mamie and Pup's lawn, where all those caught would have to stay in contact with either the tree or the hand of another caught person touching the tree. Usually the "it" team had at least two guards whose job was to keep the "caught people" caught, and not allow a free person to tag them and set them free. The hunters on the "it" team had to catch every last free person and drag them to gue before the game was over. Once every free person was caught and dragged to gue, then new sides would be determined and the game would start all over again.

These games became epic and could last for weeks at a time. Each evening we would pick up where we left off the night before.

Listen, 200 acres of woods, fields, gravel pit, backyards, sheds, garages, trees to climb, ravines, hollows, tote roads, barns, and shacks to hide in, is a lot of ground to cover if you were one of the hunters.

Especially after it was dark. It was a blast.

Of course, just before we would start a game of Monster, the older kids would tell some rousing ghost stories of bloody murders in the surrounding woods and fields to the younger kids, and as a result, they typically didn't dare wander off too far.

Made 'em easy to catch.

Hell, just let out a bloodcurdling scream, and all the young kids would come running as fast as they could, with wide eyes and thoughts of murder on their minds, to the safety of gue.

All is fair in love and war...and the game of Monster.

Another favorite game was "Army" or "War". Those 200 acres of woods, fields and gravel pit could have been used as a Hollywood set for a movie about war. It was perfect. We army men would cavort through the woods, fields and the gravel pit, crawling on our bellies in the sand, diving behind a boulder for cover, slogging through the swamp, ducking behind a tree; all the while shooting at the evil Nazi's with our guns, or throwing hand grenades (rocks) at their embankments. We became quite adept at sound effects too, from the staccato rata-tat-tat of the submachine gun, to the kapow of the grenades blowing up. I had my genuine replica toy submachine gun and army combat helmet just like Vic Morrow's on the TV show Combat, so I got to be Sergeant Saunders and lead the other kids in our attacks to kill the Nazis, and skulked around behind enemy lines.

We possessed very fertile imaginations.

One particular day when I was about seven years old, I happened to be all by myself. Pup and Unc Stub were over to The Other Farm with Unc Gene and Cuz Genie. All the neighborhood kids were busy with other things, so I found myself in the situation where I had to entertain myself.

With that "fertile imagination", that was no problem.

I decided that I was a lone army infantryman lost behind enemy lines. Only I could save the free world from the evil clutches of Nazism, if... I had "what it takes". So, I skulked and lurked about, ran through the gravel pit, ducked behind boulders, crawled on my belly in the sand, hid behind trees and killed thousands, maybe even millions, of Nazis. I blew up bridges that were critical to the Fatherland's war effort, and even took out a few of Nazi Germany's larger petrol storage facilities. From there, I had to make my escape. With hundreds ...no...thousands...maybe even millions of enraged German soldiers after me, I ran through the woods. Along the way I set traps and threw grenades back at my pursuers in the attempt to slow them down, while I searched for a way to get back to the front line and to the safety of the American troops.

Working my way through the woods and fields and then more woods, staying just minutes ahead of these million-odd Nazis, I finally popped out of the woods right behind Pup's chicken house.

There, sitting beside the chicken house, sunning herself... was Emma.

A fantastic and daring idea came to me. Yes, I had an epiphany. Emma was my means of escape from behind enemy lines.

Emma, by the way, was Pup's old '49 Dodge wooden-bodied dump truck used for hauling hay, manure, firewood, garden produce, and the many other purposes of a farm truck. For those of you that thought that the title of this story meant something entirely different...shame on you. I was a 7-year-old kid for crying out loud.

Anyway, back to the story. I ran to Emma, climbed in, "fired her up", and started driving like a madman through enemy lines, shooting out the window at Nazis along the way, ducking their return fire, swerving to miss the grenades launched at me, watching a few explode just in front of me. Whew!...that one was a close call. As I approached the front line I knew I'd have to ditch the truck, as it was a Nazi truck. I didn't want my own troops blowing me to Kingdom Come. So, I jumped out of the truck intending to run the last few feet to freedom and safety... under heavy fire, of course....when I had a second epiphany.

I needed to disable this enemy truck.

Yes, the free world was counting on me. We couldn't have those evil Germans using this truck to kill American soldiers. So, I pulled up the two folding winged flaps of the hood, and proceeded to grab every wire I could see and rip it out of the engine compartment. Pretty soon there was a pile of spark plug wires, the coil wire, and every other wire on the engine littered all over the ground around poor ol' Emma. She wasn't going anywhere soon.

Well, your little 7-year-old hero escaped the clutches of the evil Nazis....barely...and returned to a hero's welcome to the American troops on the other side of enemy lines, and the world was saved.

Later that day I was sitting at Mamie's table listening to the really cool transistor radio I had received from Dad and Mom for my birthday, and chowing down a few of Mamie's incredible molasses cookies, when Pup came home from working on The Other Farm. He mentioned that he would like me to go to work with him the following day, as there was a lot of baled hay that needed to be hauled to the barn and put in the mow.

"Sure Pup, I'll be ready to go first thing."

He said, "Good, we'll fire up Emma and head over around 7:00 am."

Uh, oh.

I took Pup out to Emma and showed him the piles of wires strewed about the front of the truck.

I was miserable. Pup looked over the scene of Emma's death, and asked me what happened. I explained, as best I could, the need to disable Emma as the free world was counting on me.

"Pup, it was those damn Germans that caused this," I reasoned.

Pup looked at me with that ever-present twinkle in his eyes, and reached over and patted me on the head, and said, "You're a good boy, Mitch."

About that time, Dad came home from work, noticed his son and his father standing beside Emma and pulled in the dooryard. He got out of his truck and sauntered up to Emma. He looked at the carnage of wires and then he looked at me. "That look" came across his face.

Yikes!

He did not pat me on the head or tell me what a good boy I was.

After a proper butt kicking and the loss of my precious transistor radio for a month, I was made to help with the resurrection of Emma. In fact, I held the drop cord light, as it took Dad and Pup several hours into the evening to put the ol' girl back together and get her running again.

I considered calling Dad a Nazi, but figured that would not be in my best interest.

I do recall that Pup and Unc Gene got a pretty good chuckle out of my little war fantasy the next day. I heard them telling the story to other older family members who shook their heads and rolled their eyes as I ran in front of Emma in the hay field. It was my job to make sure the bales of hay slid correctly into the contraption hooked on the side of the truck, which would then grab the bale with two pronged arms and lift it up and over the side of the wooden rack body.

Then Unc Stub would grab it and stack it in Emma's body, all the while teasing me about the Germans.

"Is that a harmless bale of hay, Mitch?...or a German? Better shoot it first, just in case."

I guess I had it coming.

Although my elders typically encouraged my imagination, I came to realize from "the stripping of Emma", the subsequent punishment from Dad, and the teasing from the Uncs and Pup, that one needs to separate the reality of a necessary piece of farm equipment from the fantasy of saving the world from the Nazis.

Several years later, when I was about 15, I inherited a '55 Dodge Coronet from my sister and used it as a field bomb, driving it around the farm. I was replacing the spark plugs and wires one day in front of the chicken house, when Unc Stub walked by and queried, "Saving the world from those nasty Nazis again, Mitch?"

Some lessons in life just keep on giving.....

Story Two

Saturday Night Baked Beans

It is a long-standing tradition in New England to have home-baked beans for supper on Saturday nights. This was certainly true in our family. In fact there was somewhat of a silent, but constant, competition between my grandmother, my mother, my aunt, and the wives of my uncles as to who baked the best pot of beans.

Each of these ladies had something unique about her beans... something that set hers apart from the others. My Uncle Gene's wife, Wilda, once whispered to me that her secret was the amount of dry mustard she put in the beans. Although it was never spoken, it was certainly implied that I was never, ever to breech Aunt Wilda's confidence and tell a living soul of this baked bean secret. I was no dummy, I loved her beans, and knew when to keep my mouth happily filled with her beans, and her secret locked away from "the enemy".

My dad was so impressed with my mom's baked beans that he considered turning our garage into a small baked bean factory. He thought, with baked beans that good, he stood a chance of becoming the Andrew Carnegie of the baked bean world. I was all for it, I mean being the son of the wealthiest baked bean baron in the world, plus the endless supply of baked beans seemed like a win-win situation to me. The problem was, Dad never took into account that he and Mom were on the edge of divorce and hardly ever spoke to each other.

Aunt Bev, my grandparents' only daughter, made, in Pup's words, "A damn fine bean." Aunt Brenda, Unc Stub's wife, was no slouch either, her beans always got "good reports", as Unc Stub was fond of saying.

The queen bean baker, though, was my grandmother. Mamie's beans were always perfect, not too hard, not mushy, not too sweet, but not dry either. In fact, it was Mamie who gave me her own little trade secret in the art of bean baking: add a chunked up smoked sausage to the pot about two hours before the beans are done baking, for that slightly smoky flavor that really makes the beans something akin to baked bean nirvana.

Another thing that set my grandmothers beans apart from the others was her homemade biscuits.

Oh my!

You can't have baked beans without homemade biscuits. If it isn't illegal, it damn sure ought to be. Now, I am not saying that the other ladies didn't make a "damn fine biscuit" because they most assuredly did. Biscuits to die for, but, consider this little fact, my grandmother, by my calculations, made well over 750,000 biscuits in her life. That's a lot of biscuits.

No one could make biscuits like Mamie, they would almost float in midair they were so light and flaky, smeared with homemade butter from Pup's butter-churn, and dipped in the bean juice is pretty close to baked bean heaven.

Accompanying the baked beans and biscuits was my grandfather's homemade sauerkraut. Pup made two 30-gallon crocks of 'kraut every fall when we would harvest countless heads of cabbage from his garden. The "Making of the 'Kraut" each fall was a spectacular event in my childhood and so I will devote another entire story chronicling this most reverent of traditions.

So, sitting around my grandparents' table, in their kitchen, in the farmhouse I grew up in, on a typical Saturday night, were my grandparents, my parents, my uncles and their wives, my aunt and her husband, and all my cousins--between 12 to 18 people, depending. To this day, I don't know how that was managed, but it was, and on a regular basis.

Besides all those people, who were practically drooling over the smell of baked beans and hot biscuits wafting through the kitchen, was the food.

Huge mounds of sauerkraut in bowls, platters piled high with biscuits, other bowls filled with steaming hot-dogs, small crocks of homemade butter, and others filled with homemade jam, and of course, large two-gallon crocks of baked beans, fresh from the oven. It was an orgy of unbelievable proportions, a flurry of ladles of beans being doled out into plates, biscuits being smeared with the butter and/or jam, 'kraut being piled on the plate beside the beans, and hot-dogs being dumped on top...all to the sound of 18 people talking, laughing, and groaning in anticipation.

It was beautiful.

After everyone was gorged, the men would retire to the living room for a smoke and for storytelling, while the womenfolk would clean up the remains, and do the dishes, while having their own version of storytelling. We kids would flitter back and forth trying to decipher who had the juiciest story to listen to.

One particular Saturday, after we all had waddled from the table, completely sated and holding our bellies, the men settled into the living room. Pup sat in his overstuffed rocker beside the window, Unc Gene was in the recliner across from him, Dad and Unc Stub were holding down the sofa, while Uncle Roy was in the overstuffed wing back chair by the TV. We kids squeezed in where we could, cousin Genie-bub was in-between Unc Stub and Dad on the sofa, I was sitting on the floor with my back against the wall beside the sofa, while cousins Randy and Robbie were fighting over who was gonna sit on the padded chest that held my grandmother's Electrolux.

My sis and cousin Linda were out in the kitchen helping with the cleanup chores and adding to the buzz of conversation out there. Both Pup and Unc Gene pulled out their rolling papers and a foil pack of Prince Edward tobacco and rolled themselves a smoke, Dad filled his pipe while Unc Stub tickled cousin Genie-bub.

Just as we were settling in and a hush came over the living room in anticipation of a story, Pup cocked his leg and let a very loud and very long fart reverberate through the living room. The cousins and I started to laugh, the Uncs and Dad looked a bit envious....and.....the kitchen became deathly silent.

My grandmother appeared in the doorway between the kitchen and living room. She was glaring at Pup and spoke in that voice that typically meant someone was in trouble, "Henry Littlefield!...you STOP that!"

"Well, Mother," says Pup with a little self-satisfied smirk on his face, "perhaps you better stop it....it's heading your way."

The cousins and I were doubled over holding our bellies laughing, the Uncs and Dad were laughing but trying to keep Mamie from seeing them do so, even the rest of the ladies in the kitchen were snickering and covering their grins with their hands. Mamie started making that little "tch tch tch" noise that indicated her disapproval, but I think I saw the smallest hint of a smile on her face, too. After a few minutes we got ourselves under control and Pup began to tell us all a story.

It was a story of how he ran away from home when he was all of 14 years old, along with his older brother, how they had slept in the hay mow of a farmer's barn where they could look out through the holes in the roof and count the stars, where the temperature was often below freezing. He told us how he and his brother had to work for the farmer to earn the right to sleep in his barn and to get three meals a day. He went on to explain that work included cutting timber and firewood and hauling it out of the woods by horse-drawn scoots, of mucking out the barn and tending to the farmer's animals, and on occasion, when the work was caught up, how they would take the farmers hounds and go rabbit hunting.

It was a heck of an adventure and none of us ever tired of these stories from my grandfather's life.

After the story, after the kitchen was cleaned, and all the dishes were washed and put away in the cupboards, everyone prepared to go home. There were the hugs and kisses from the women, the pats on the shoulder from the men, of course the pinches on the butt between the cousins and me, and within 15 minutes the house was empty, except for Mamie and Pup.

The rest of this story was told to me by my grandmother. She always claimed that this was one of her favorite recollections.

After the family had left to go to their own homes and beds, Pup, as he usually did, went to bed early. He would be up at 4:00 am the next morning to prepare for his day. Mamie stayed up for a while and watched TV, probably Lawrence Welk, that was one of her favorites. Mamie and Pup's bedroom was right off the living room and Mamie could hear Pup snoring away.

After she had watched TV for a while she decided to go to bed too. She shook Pup as she crawled into bed with him, "Henry...roll over and stop snoring."

Pup just grunted in his sleep and went back to a lusty snore, punctuated, by one resounding fart after another. Mamie starting putting the elbows to Pup, trying to get him to wake up. She said, just as she was yelling at him, " Henry!...you have GOT to stop snoring...I can't sleep...and YOU HAVE GOT TO STOP passing gas....it stinks something awful!!" that she took a cramp herself...and let one slide out.

Yes, the ole SBD, (silent but deadly).

About that time Pup was half awake, clearing his throat, he sat up in bed took a couple of big whiffs, and remarked, "By God, Mother...them do stink, don't they?"

Pup immediately rolled over and went back to sleep, Mamie said she laid awake most of the night laughing. Nothing like them Saturday night baked beans.

Story Three

Morning Glory

It was the summer of 1969. In fact it was the first day after school was out. I was blissful in my sleep that morning, dreaming of all the adventures this 13-year-old was going to have on the farm over the summer, when this distant voice intruded through the depth of my slumber and popped the dream bubble in my head.

"Time to get up, Mitch, I am heading over to The Other Farm to get some mushrooms, five minutes!"

My grandfather, hollering from the foot of the stairs, had plans that didn't include me lazing in bed all day. I pried my eyes open and bleary-eyed my watch.

4:30 a.m.

It wasn't even full daylight yet.

Then I remembered the mention of The Other Farm and mushrooms, and I knew what that meant! I piled out of bed, ran to the bathroom, did my business, hot-footed it back to my room, pulled on some jeans, my sneakers and a t-shirt, then scampered down the stairs to the kitchen where Pup was sitting at the table with a cup of coffee, reading the latest edition of The Grit....four minutes flat. Ha!

I grinned at my grandfather.

"Sounds like a great idea to me, Pup....need some help?"

He chuckled and looked at me with the ever-present twinkle in his blue eyes, "I could probably use a little. Don't s'pose you'd be willing to drive me over, would ya?"

My grandfather knew that like all boys who were approaching teen-hood, I craved every opportunity I got to drive any of the farm equipment, and considered it a real coup indeed to be allowed to drive the pickup from one farm to the other, over the public roads. It was one of a thousand "passages of manhood", so to speak. It was something that every boy dreamed of doing. It was also illegal. I wasn't even quite 13 yet. My birthday was a month away. It would be another four years before I garnered my Maine state driver's license.

Made it all that more irresistible.

I also knew that a quick trip to The Other Farm to gather mushrooms meant my favorite breakfast was on tap.

Venison backstrap sauteed with butter, garlic, and mushrooms. A few fried potatoes, and Pup's drop biscuits, which he referred to as "door-stops", was a meal fit for a king, or a farmboy.

So, Pup headed out through the shed, stopped to grab his sage green Dickies cap, then we wandered out to the driveway where his old 1956 Ford sat. The truck was once dark blue but had faded to a rusty blue/brown, and the bed of the truck had been replaced by a wooden body with wooden rack sides that were five feet tall. Didn't want the assortment of farm animals that were occasionally hauled in the truck to get "any ideas" so the rack sides were tall enough so they would feel enclosed.

We climbed into the ol' girl, Pup on the passenger side, me behind the wheel. Even at almost 13, I was fairly tall, so I could reach the pedals and see over the steering wheel at the same time, but the whole idea of pushing the clutch and shifting the gears was where my inexperience showed. After several attempts to back the truck up, which damn near caused whiplash for both Pup and I, I was able to get turned around and headed down the driveway, a-lurching and a-jerking every inch of the way until I hit the road where the truck and I became one.

Well, at least the truck wasn't shaking like a dog shitting razor blades anymore and Pup was able to take his hand off his cap.

"Now, that is one way to get a man's blood a-flowing," Pup commented. "And," he added, "You didn't hit anything."

I had a grin from ear to ear, but didn't dare to take my eyes from the road to see if Pup was okay. I was thrilled. I managed to get into fourth gear and had the ol' girl racing down the road at 30 miles per hour. I even did fairly well down-shifting to take the almost 180-degree turn from our road onto the Poors Mills road which led to The Other Farm without much problem. Of course it was downhill, so that helped. In a few short minutes we were wheeling into the driveway of The Other Farm where we lurched to a stop, a few yards short of the gate into the pasture, beside the barn.

I managed to get the truck through the gate with a couple of backfires and lurches, stopping so Pup could get back in after he closed the gate. Perhaps it was just my imagination but he seemed a little reluctant to climb back aboard. In fact, he suggested we walk to the area of the pasture where the ground was littered with white button mushrooms.

I stepped out of the truck to join my grandfather and took in the scene before me. It was nothing short of amazing. We were facing east and the sun was starting to rise, creating the long shadows of early morning. The land in front of us sloped downward to a valley, which at its lowest point, held a babbling brook. The neon green grass of the fields was punctuated by the iridescent yellow of thousands of dandelions, and further illustrated by the puffs of white wool, and the abstract pattern of black and white cowhide as the sheep and the Holstein cows milled aimlessly about, nibbling the tender green grasses. I could hear the mournful cry of a mourning dove, and the beginnings of the daytime sounds of nature as another summer day in rural Maine came to be. As we meandered down the slope to the area where the mushrooms had always grown in abundance, drinking in the beauty of our surroundings, the bucolic moment was assaulted by the harsh bitching of a couple of crows. Mouthy creatures to be sure. I remarked, "Damned old crows...always making a racket."

Pup's eyes twinkled as he replied, "I think they may be warning the other critters you that were driving."

We both laughed at this, as he patted my shoulder and pointed to a patch of button mushrooms standing proudly about 20 feet in front of us. Using our pocket knives, we started to clip them at the base and put them in a paper bag. We didn't take long, within 10 minutes we both had our bags better than half full. Pup always said,

"Don't take more than you're gonna eat. Ma Nature will preserve them better than our refrigerator."

We walked back to the truck, and it was not spoken but understood that Pup would drive home. I was happy, I was out of school for the summer, and I'd had the chance to drive over. I got to see the sun coming up over what I thought was the most beautiful place on earth, and I was in for a treat for breakfast. Life was good. Who could complain?

So, we drove back to Pup's farm, with him putt-putting along at a robust speed of, oh say...15mph, waving at the one other early morning vehicle as it passed. It happened to be a neighboring farmer, Harry Copson. Pup remarked, "Harry must be headed over to Bowen's, only place open this time of day."

Bowen's was a little ramshackle country store located about two miles from both Harry's and our farms, and it was indeed open every morning at 5:00 a.m. Bowen's was the place to go if you were of the farming community in and around the west Belfast countryside.

At this point my belly was growling and I was day-dreaming about back strap and biscuits. We finally made it back to the homestead and lugged nature's bounty inside. I brushed the mushrooms clean with a small paint brush used specifically for this purpose. Never wash mushrooms in water. Pup, meanwhile, was preparing his drop biscuits and had sliced up some of last night's leftover supper potatoes and pelted them with salt and pepper. Next he laid them in a skillet with some home-churned butter, and adjusted the knob on the stove so the pan was sizzling slightly. Gotta be careful with the temperature, butter burns easily.

He dropped large gobs of goo that comprised his biscuit mix on a cookie sheet and shoved them in the oven and then he began to prepare this morning's entree. He sliced the tenderloin about 3/4-inch thick, creating little butterfly steaks, sprinkled a bit of pepper and garlic powder on them, then sliced the mushrooms and pelted them with salt and pepper, and a bit more garlic powder. He laid this all in another huge black cast iron skillet which was just coming to the perfect temp and the butter was just starting to bubble. The kitchen was beginning to smell really good and my belly began to growl even louder.

About this time, my grandmother, Mamie, came into the kitchen to prepare herself a morning cup of tea, some toast, and receive a hug from her grandson. As she always did when Pup cooked, she wrinkled her nose and asked, "Henry, what stinks?"

"Must be my feet, Mother."

I chuckled, Mamie snickered, and she went to the stove to snag a piece of potato to nibble on and gave Pup a smile and a quick hug. She then took her tea and toast to the living room to enjoy with the morning news on TV.

Mamie was beloved by not only her entire brood, but by everyone that knew her. She was truly a mother who nurtured each and every one who spent time with her. And, she was an incredible cook like most ladies of her generation. But, she had a nose like a bloodhound, and she would often make my grandfather cook out in the shed on a hot plate if he cooked something she found offensive to her oh-so sensitive nose. This particular morning, I think she was pulling his leg a little, but she didn't use garlic and usually complained about the smell of it cooking when he did. Fish was out of the question, but she loved to eat fish. Go figure.

About this time, which was all of 5:30 a.m., my father and my uncle Stubby walked in. They typically would join Pup for breakfast before my dad would head to his job, and Unc Stub would head to the chicken houses to start his day on the farm. They looked a bit bleary-eyed and were customarily quiet until they had a cup or two of coffee to get their systems going. They smelled what Pup was cooking and that seemed to rouse them, but perhaps it was that initial jolt of caffeine. As we all chatted over the coffee, Pup began to dole out helpings on the plates sitting in front of each of us at the kitchen table. First came the potatoes, perfectly browned and slightly crispy, sizzling with the homemade butter they were cooked in. Then a large serving bowl of the steaming hot biscuits was set on the table beside the small bowl of Pup's own home-churned butter, and a jar of Mamie's raspberry preserves. Finally, Pup carried the large skillet containing the tenderloin and mushrooms around the table, shuffling off a helping for each of us with his spatula. Coffee cups were filled and then we all proceeded to eat this incredible breakfast, enjoying the company, the conversation, and the food.

These moments were snippets of time that we all looked forward to then, and the memories now of those mornings in my grandparents' kitchen with them, and other family members are still cherished by all of us who survive today. We often reminisce about those days when we are together at family gatherings these days, and breakfast with Mamie and Pup are always some of the favorite memories.

Story Four

Donkey Daze

Living on a farm allows for a lot of diversity, in fact it demands diversity. Each day is a new adventure wrapped around the same basic duties and responsibilities. Therefore it is important for the farm family to be flexible to accommodate the needs of the farm, its family members, its animal population, its land and buildings and equipment, and its produce and product. One day a farm family may be planning on getting the gardens ready for planting, but one or more of the animals may demand more than usual attention, so one has to be able to go with the flow and live with the priorities. Because of this, the typical farmer tends to have a very basic and practical, some might even say "earthy", view of life.

Living on the farm offers an almost condensed version of the life cycle we humans experience. Living among and tending a variety of animal's daily needs allowed me to experience many amazing things when I was a kid growing up. From the most basic bodily functions to watching the miracle of new life when that lamb or that calf first came into this world. We had a herd of about 250 sheep, which meant that every spring we would have about 300 lambs born. Typically sheep have twins, sometimes a single, sometimes a set of triplets, on rare occasion, more. We also would have a few calves born from the small herd of heifers we raised. I watched a foal come into this world, and I've seen puppies, kittens, and kids (goats) born many times. I've watched countless eggs crack and become a little puff of golden peach fuzz that peeps and scurries about.

I've even had to help with some of these births.

Yes...a de facto wet nurse for sheep.

Most of my family had this experience more than once. It was not uncommon for a sheep to become breech and when you're 9-10 years old, your arm tends to be much smaller in diameter than the Popeye arms of my grandfather and uncles. The idea was to help the lamb turn in the proper position without injuring it, or the mother. You might be amazed at how sharp those little hooves can be.

Sometimes it helped...other times we might lose the lamb. Other times we might lose the mother sheep. Always a disappointment, and always sad, but a fact of life on the farm. On those occasions when the lamb was born and survived, but the mother did not, typically one of us kids would become the lamb's "mother". We would nurse it with a baby's bottle until it was grown enough to be able to fend for itself.

All part of the life cycle.

Of course, I was also there when we would put the bulls in with the heifers, or, the rams in with the ewes during the "in season". What transpired over the next three or four days was beyond amazing. Naturally, it was an event that was viewed with a lot of commentary and even some side bets on one's favorite...uh..."stud". Suffice to say, four rams to service 250-300 ewes in a three to four-day period was, well... inspirational.

I told you we had an "earthy" view of life.

Of course, this earthy attitude was fairly prevalent in the locker room at school when I was a teenager too. My cousin, Genie, and I were the butt of a lot of good-natured, let's call them, off-color jokes and jibes because we were farm boys.

"Hey, Littlefield, I drove past your farm the other night and saw all those baby lambs....two or three of them really resemble you. You must be really proud...not passing out cigars are you?"

Hardy...har har.

Or the classic....."Is that sheep with the blue ribbon on its neck your prom date, Littlefield?"

Another knee-slapper.

Another source of smirks and jokes from the peanut gallery at school was our donkey. The donkey was named "Ed Muskie", after Maine's famous political son. Ed Muskie was a friendly little donkey, very docile, and if one was hard up enough and really didn't want to walk to the creek to fish, you could ride him. He didn't mind really, but he was a terrible ride. He loved cigarettes, and he loved apples, so he was likely to pester anyone in the pasture for a treat. He also had one other "colorful" habit as well.

Any time someone new, someone he wasn't used to seeing regularly, would come to the farm, Ed Muskie loved to show just how excited he was to see a potential new friend.

I mean "excited" in its most basic form.

He was an extremely well-hung donkey.

Yes, ol' Ed would come to the edge of the pasture, closest to the house, when anyone would pull into the driveway, or if these unfamiliar people happened to go into the pasture, he would go up and greet them, usually very excited to see them.

You get the picture.

Anyway, I've always found it a bit amusing that certain subject matter isn't appropriate to discuss in certain settings, except in the boys locker room at high school, of course, such as, one doesn't usually talk about religion and sex at the same time. Depending on the individual, one or both of those two subjects is always taboo.

Which brings me to the Jehovah's Witnesses.

Now, I should point out that my family, myself included, has always respected anyone's faith and their religion, so I'm not singling out JWs. It just so happens they are the folks that commonly came door to door to discuss their faith, when I was a kid, and in fact they still do. I have a couple that comes to my home from time to time and we have interesting discussions. They are a fine young couple, and I enjoy our discussions.

Most of the men in my family tend to be quite introspective and keep their faith in their God to themselves, while some of the women-folk were a bit more demonstrative regarding religion. Back in those days, Morrill Baptist Church was filled each Sunday with farm families, including some of my aunts and cousins, and myself occasionally too.

In any case, when the JWs would come door to door, word was passed rather quickly down the line to the neighbors to prepare for their visit. Sort of a Paul Revere-esque type of thing...if you get my drift.

Unc Stub chuckles about the time he was helping his older brother Warren, my dad, dig his cellar out. Unc Stub was about 14 at the time, and Dad would have been about 28. Dad lived just down and across the road from Mamie and Pup's farm. Unc Stub crawled out of the muck and clay of the hole under the house to get a drink of water, it was very hot, and the work was very difficult, so lots of fluids were needed to keep going. As he climbed out of the hole he spied two women in their Sunday best standing on the front doorstep of Mamie's house, talking with her. He immediately knew what was going on. First, one never ever uses the front door of the house, unless you're company. Secondly, these two ladies were dressed for, well...church.

Dead giveaway.

So, Unc Stub knew they would be heading their way in a few minutes after my grandmother talked with them and took their reading materials. So he ran back and warned Dad.

"War...the Holy Rollers are at Mother's....they gonna be heading this way in a minute."

Yes, I know, Jehovah's Witnesses are not "Holy Rollers", but my family called them that. I don't know why...they just did.

So, Dad says, "Come with me."

He and Unc Stub go into his house, shirtless, sweat rolling down their faces and bare chests, which are also covered in mud and muck, and Dad proceeds to pull a 6-pack of beer out of the fridge and snaps one open, takes a healthy swig, and he waits.

Sure enough, a couple minutes later the two ladies walk up to Dad's door and knock. Dad says, "C'mon in."

The two women walked into the house to find this man and this teenager standing there shirtless, dripping sweat and mud, the man slugging from a bottle of beer, and Dad hollers, "Well, hello baby!...Have a beer!"

Unc Stub said the two women's eyes went wide, their jaws dropped and they began a frantic attempt to get past one another in the effort to get out the door while Dad hollered a parting, "God bless you," to their backsides.

Dad is a classy guy.

Another time we were in the middle of hay season, which meant it was July. I was about 15 at the time. It was lunch time, and Pup, Unc Gene, Genie, Aunt Wilda's brother, Rocky, and I were sitting on Unc Gene's picnic table on his front lawn eating cucumber sandwiches and drinking iced tea, when a car pulled into the driveway and three folks dressed in their Sunday best got out.

One man and two women.

They started to approach us and Unc Gene said, "You folks should probably go and knock on the door and speak to my wife. We are just getting ready to head back into the hayfield...gotta get those bales in before it rains."

There wasn't a cloud in the sky.

But they got the message and proceeded to step up on the porch just as Aunt Wilda stepped out with her bible in her hands.

Good Morrill Baptist that she was, she was prepared to debate the finer points of salvation.

Remember the donkey?

Oh yes, Ed Muskie came up to the edge of the pasture at a hot trot, and was his typically "excited" self.

It was just a question of when the "Holy Rollers" happened to notice.

It may have been the fact that Rocky and I were doubled over laughing and pointing at Ed that gave it away.

Genie-bub was laughing too but trying not to make a scene; Pup was smirking and watching, as was Unc Gene. It was one of the ladies in the group that first noticed why we were having such a fit over on the picnic table and she immediately went scarlet. The man and the other woman started to look around to see the source of her discomfort and they both started to stare at ol' Ed Muskie, and the three of them started to back up and head for their car. Meanwhile, Aunt Wilda, who was used to ol' Ed's tricks never paid it a mind and was still trying to get a theological point across to the three highly embarrassed laymen. I can tell you it didn't take them long to get in their car and move along.

I've always wondered what the conversation in that car was, right after that incident.

Ed seemed a bit...well...deflated, after they left, probably figuring he had lost out on a cigarette. Aunt Wilda just shook her head in annoyance at us and went back into the house, as we continued to laugh and get ready to go back into the hayfield.

Before we did, I bummed a Pall Mall from Unc Gene and went over and fed it to Ed Muskie and gave him a nice scratch between his ears. I thought he had earned it.

Story Five

The Making of the Kraut

Life on the farm offers a plethora of experiences due to the nature of the work and responsibilities. One must become adept at dealing with almost every possible situation that will sooner or later arise and, as important, farm life is dictated by financial constraints. A farm family must become as self-sustaining as possible. The farm family typically raises all of its meat--beef, pork, lamb, chicken (which also provides eggs), turkey, and duck. The clever farmer also knows all the prime spots to hunt deer, partridge, rabbit, and pheasant, as well as the best spots to catch trout, salmon, bass, white perch, and alewives (a shad-like fish that spawn in coastal Maine streams and which are caught and then smoked). Also, we would often go saltwater fishing for mackerel, striped bass, and blue fish, as well as dig for clams during the low tide. We not only raised and hunted this meat and fish; we also butchered, cut, and wrapped all the meat for our freezers. Not much went to waste. We didn't eat just steaks, although we ate steak...oh no...there was liver, heart, tongue, and tripe too.

Mmmmm...tripe. The lining of a cows stomach...or perhaps you would prefer some Rocky Mountain oysters?...oh yes...we ate them too. Wanna come over for dinner?

If you do, you should be aware of our "golden rule"... you eat what is put on the table and be thankful for it.

Settle down...it isn't that bad.

Anyway, at times we would sometimes sell "1/2 of a critter" to provide some income, which meant that when we butchered, we would also butcher enough to sell to a few regular customers.

Moving right along, the farmer also raises a huge garden, or more aptly put, several gardens.

There was the main vegetable gardens in which the typical veggies are raised--peas, lettuce, Swiss chard, peppers, beets/beet greens, carrots, squash (summer, butternut, buttercup, zucchini), tomato (several types for eating and canning/stewing), beans (bush beans, yellow eyes for baked beans, pole beans, lima), cucumbers, corn (three types, early maturity, later maturity, and a less starchy for freezing), potato (three types, red as they are early, russets for bakers, and green mountains for wintering), parsnips, turnip, radishes, celery, onions, broccoli, cauliflower, cabbage (red and white), and horseradish (to make horseradish sauce...an eye-watering experience, but oh so good) and more I'm sure I've forgotten.

There were the herbs, usually raised along the sill of the house as it provided protection and warmth--dill, tarragon, sage, chive, basil to name a few.

There was a separate garden for the strawberries, a raspberry patch, and a rhubarb patch.

We had apple orchards, the summer apples of Golden Delicious, Yellow Transparent, and Granny Smith, but also Wolf River and Mac for wintering.

"Makes a damn fine pie."

We had bee hives for the honey.

Pup, the Uncs and Dad knew all the best spots to dig dandelion greens in the spring, as well as where the fiddleheads were plentiful. Pup would harvest mushrooms from the fields on the farm, white button mushrooms to be sautéed in butter, onions and garlic...oh my! They knew where to go to get the best wild blackberries. We also made our own maple syrup by tapping the rock Maples on our farm.

We made our own butter in an old fashioned hand-cranked butter churn, from the milk we got from our milk cows.

The freezing, canning, stewing, pickling and preserving of all that our gardens and Mother Nature had to offer was a big job. Hundreds of jars of pickles of many varieties--bread and butter, sour, sweet, dill, corn relish, tomato relish, pickled beets, pickled green beans, and pickled fiddleheads. Hundreds more jars of canned green beans, stewed tomatoes, canned fiddleheads, and canned carrots. Bags of frozen sweet corn, Swiss chard, beet greens, rhubarb, and peas. Barrels of apples for the winter in the cellar, bushel upon bushel of potatoes, mesh bags of onions, turnip, and squash. Bundles of yellow eye beans drying, ready to be thrashed for baking beans. Jars of honey, and maple syrup, jars of apple jelly, homemade strawberry, raspberry, and blackberry jams. Jars of horseradish sauce.

We always ate biscuits and bread hot and fresh from the oven. Apple pies, apple crisp, raspberry and blackberry pies, mincemeat pies, molasses cookies, oatmeal and raisin cookies, were always available and always fresh out of the oven.

Enough to make a fella's belly growl, ain't it?

Yes, we ate very well, but it was hours of work to accomplish all this. The women-folk worked feverishly doing all the freezing, canning, pickling, and preserving in an attempt to keep up with all the produce we men-folk would haul in from the gardens and forages.

Plus, these ladies did all the cooking and baking for a very large family who ate like they worked.

There's nothing like the smell of apple pie in the oven when you come in from the fields for supper.

The ladies in my family were all outstanding cooks and it didn't matter to me whose table I sat at to eat, because I knew I was in for a treat.

But, even these ladies, who were so adept at making hearty meals that would make you moan in appreciation when you ate, from time to time would make a "boo-boo".

Aunt Bev chuckles when she recalls the time she and Unc Mo sat down with Pup at Mamie's table, one cold winter night, for a supper of biscuits and corn chowder. Mamie served them and then as they ate, she, as was common, busied herself with cleaning. (Mamie rarely sat at the table to eat with her children unless it was a large family gathering.) So, Aunty begins to spoon some of the chowder…it was rich and creamy, lotsa potato and onion…hmmmm…no yellow of the corn kernels…strange…Unc Mo notices the same thing and asks Aunt Bev, "Is this fish chowder?"

Pup responded, "This here is poor man's soup."

Mamie overheard the exchange, looked puzzled for a moment, and then started laughing. She looked over on the cupboard and noticed a bowl full of corn she had taken out of the freezer to make the chowder from, she had forgotten to put it in the pot!

Pup, being the gentleman, baled Mamie out, "Best damn potato and onion soup I've ever had, Mother."

So anyway, we as a family spent a fair amount of time involving ourselves in all facets of our food. My favorite of these responsibilities was "the making of the 'kraut."

Every fall we would harvest hundreds of heads of cabbage from our gardens. Sometimes if we didn't raise enough, we would buy more heads from neighboring farmers who had more than they needed. We then would pile all these heads on Unc Gene's porch and on tarps laid out in front of the porch where the sun was the warmest. It was important to let the heads dry for a few days as it wouldn't do to have any water in them.

Then, after the heads were properly dried, we would start cutting. It was a production line of sorts. I would grab a head and toss it to Unc Gene standing over a large cutting board, who would take his large butcher knife and chop the head in two and remove the stem, he would then drop the two halves into a bucket. Cousin Genie would take the bucket of cabbage head halves over to Pup who was standing over the cabbage shredder, which was set up on two carpenter "hosses". The cabbage shredder was a flat board affair about three feet long and a foot and a half wide. It had a series of blades in the middle with a rack that rode back and forth on the inside. Pup would put a few of the cabbage heads in the rack and start pushing it back and forth and the shredded cabbage would fall from the blades into a five-gallon bucket sitting underneath.

We always did this on a warm sunny fall day in Unc Gene's yard, in front of his porch. People driving by would gawk at this scene and wonder what in hell we were doing. Others who KNEW what we were doing honked their horns and waved, they knew it meant that we were making sauerkraut.

Still, for the uninitiated, it must have presented quite the scene...some kid throwing cabbages at a guy with a butcher's knife, who was whacking 'em up like a hibachi chef on steroids...another kid hauling a bushel basket of cut cabbage heads over to an older gentleman who was pushing this board back and forth lustily while shredded cabbage was flying through the air. In the front yard, of all places!

If the Jehovah's Witnesses happened by on that day, they would drive right by the house without stopping.

As far as I know, we were never reported to the police.

After this fun little exercise we would end up with all these five-gallon buckets of shredded cabbage. Then, we would go down in Unc's cellar and haul out these two 30-gallon clay crocks and wash and rinse them out. We then set up operations inside of Unc's woodshed.

This was the part where my stomach would start growling in anticipation, and I'd get "that look" from Unc.

"You know nephew, it's gonna be eight weeks or so before this is gonna be ready to eat."

"I know Unc...I know...can't wait."

"Well, ok then...try and not drool in the cabbage."

So, Unc would take this "tamper", which was made from a stick of firewood. It had been drilled on one end to fit a 4-foot handle into it. Unc would mash down the shredded cabbage inside the crocks as Pup would toss some in, throw in a handful of cabbage, an occasional healthy pinch of sea salt, and tamp. Repeat. After a while, both crocks would be filled with this condensed, pounded, shredded cabbage and sea salt. We would then, very carefully, lug the two crocks back down cellar and place them over in the corner away from the wood furnace and cover them with a 1/2-inch thick clay cover that sat inside the crock, then cover that with a towel.

It took about eight weeks for the kraut to "work", basically pickle, and then we would have to test it, of course, to see if it needed more time.

The finished product was this sauerkraut that was incredible. It would be crisp, yet not fresh. It would have the perfect flavor—a nice tang, but not too sour. It was the perfect complement to many meals, baked beans especially, but it was fantastic on a ham sandwich, too.

Over the course of the winter, the family would work on those two 30-gallon crocks stored in Unc Gene's cellar, so it meant that he was getting visits from family members a lot. My dad would go over to Unc's with my little brother to get two Tupperware bowls of kraut at a time, one to have in the fridge to go with meals or sandwiches, and the other to eat on the way home in the car.

I still to this day eat a lot of kraut, but it is "store bought", made at a farm in Washington, Maine. It is good, real good, but it doesn't compare to the kraut we made.

I think ours was so much better because we made it ourselves.

Story Six

Memories of Shucking Peas

One day when I was in my early 20s, I decided to go visit my dad. You see, my dad had just gone through his fourth divorce and his third wife.

Yes, his fourth divorce and third wife. He married my mother twice.

He and my mom married when they were teenagers and had my sister. After about four years, they parted ways, and Dad immediately married another lady. That union lasted about a year, and they divorced. Dad and Mom then decided to give it another shot....so to speak. While many folks thought they were probably crazy to try again, I am particularly glad they did.

I was born about nine months later.

When I was twelve Mom and Dad realized those folks who called them crazy for ever marrying twice, were right, and divorced yet again.

Wait...I ain't done yet.

Then Dad married a gal who was four months older than my sister. Yes, he was quite cocky about it too. That marriage lasted about ten years before history repeated itself.

Which brings me to my little story.

In spite of his experience level, I kinda figured Dad to be a little down after his fourth divorce, so I tried to spend as much time with him as I could. This particular day was a Saturday; I went over to his house to see what he was up to and to offer to help him with his chores. He informed me he was walking up to visit Mamie, his mother. He allowed I could tag along as long as I didn't eat all of her molasses cookies like the pig I was. After a bit of negotiations, we agreed that I could have four molasses cookies. My grandparents lived across the road from Dad on the family farm, so it was a short walk, fortunately, as my belly was growling and my mind was now on my grandmother's incredible molasses cookies.

Dad must have heard my belly growling because he shot "that look" at me...y'know, the look one has right after he steps where the dog fertilized the lawn.

I smiled and held up four fingers, indicating our deal. Dad shook his head in defeat and walked around the corner of the shed to enter Mamie's house.

In our family one always uses the shed door to enter the house. If there is no shed you are to use the back door. The front door is never ever used, except for company, and there are no exceptions to this rule. I think this is a time-honored tradition which speaks of my family's need to wear their blue collar roots as a merit badge, but when I pontificated this thought to my dad once, he just gave me "that look", and wondered, I'm sure, why he married my mother the second time.

Anyway, we walked around the corner of the shed, and there was my grandfather sitting on the shed steps in the shade shucking a bushel basket of fresh peas from his garden. He greeted us in his usual manner—a nod of the head and a dry, "Well now, the things you see when you ain't carrying a gun."

I said, "Hey Pup...listen, I gotta go grab me a handful or two...I mean...four of Mamie's cookies, and I'll come back out and give you a hand."

My dad says, "I'm gonna go in and see Mother for a minute, then I'll come back out and help you with those peas." He glared at me once more for good measure, and walked up the steps and into the shed.

My grandfather chuckled, "Don't 'spect you'll be long."

I followed Dad through the shed into Mamie's kitchen and lo and behold, what do we find?

There, sitting around my grandmothers table, were three women. My grandmother, of course, and the others were two of Dad's ex-wives. My mother and the woman my father had just recently divorced looked up and smiled at me. Realizing the possibility of a "golden moment" I smiled at them all, hugs and kisses all around, and then proceeded to the Tupperware bowl in the cupboard where the cookies were stashed.

My father, who is fairly good at connecting the dots, immediately realized he didn't stand a chance, even with my help. He turned on his heel and hotfooted it back to the safety of the shed steps and my grandfather.

As I ate three or four cookies the women informed me that Mom was in town for a week or so and would be staying there with my grandparents, and Diane, the most recent of Dad's divorces, was also staying there for the night. I loved my grandparents for this simple way of looking at life and family. Dad may have divorced these two, but they hadn't, so like the rest of the family, the ladies were welcome to stay as long as they liked.

Taking four more cookies, I bade the ladies adieu, and headed out to the shed steps for a little pea shucking.

My grandfather and my father were sitting side by side shucking peas, not saying a word.

I figured it was time to inject a little conversation into the situation so I said, "Heh, you were right Pup, that didn't take him long did it?"

Dad started to shuck peas with a noticeable upbeat in intensity.

Pup replied with a twinkle in his eyes. "Y'know, seems your Dad has just enough to get a woman…not quite enough to keep one."

I laughed. Meanwhile Dad must have been trying to get into the Guinness Book of World Records in the 'speed pea-shucking' category, so I tried to be helpful by saying, "Well Pup, it's nice you have all those ladies staying with you, eh?"

Pup says, "He-yuh, if I had any more sons like him, I'd have to sell the farm and buy a hotel."

At this point even Dad started laughing. I mean….this was seriously funny stuff.

The three of us, grandfather, son, and grandson spent the next hour on those old cement steps that led to my grandparents shed, shucking peas, good naturedly ribbing my Dad, drinking a couple cold beers, enjoying the sounds of summer, and each other's company. It was a moment in time the three of us cherished.

I think the three of us realized that, even while it was transpiring, we were experiencing a special moment in each of our lives that remains forever part of who we are and what we become. In spite of the hardships we are all subject to in our life's journey, there are those golden "memories of shucking peas" in each of our lives, which keep us and sustain us. I can tell you that this little story is one of my fondest memories of the three of us together; it never fails to remind me of the importance of humor, the love of our family, and the ability to laugh at yourself.

Story Seven

Bad Blood

Growing up as part of a farming family meant that when we recreated, it usually was in a form that would also be somehow productive to the farming way of life. For example, if we kids wanted to go ice skating, the men would tag along to ice fish. So, we would build a bon-fire on the shore for warmth and for cooking, shovel off an area to ice skate on, while the men would auger out holes in the ice and set the traps. This was great fun. We got to fish and ice skate, enjoy hot-dogs and melted cheese on a piece of wonder bread, cooked over an open fire, and listen to stories and yarns from the elders. From the elders' perspective, this was a way to let us boys and girls have a little fun while at the same time garnering a little of ol' Ma Nature's offerings for the dinner table, and for the freezer, while at the same time they had fun. Even crusty ol' farmers like to have fun y'know.

At other times, we would go bass or trout fishing in the spring and summer for the same purpose.

We would go saltwater fishing for mackerel, and at the same time go clamming. We would go fiddle-heading. We knew all the best spots to find wild blackberries, raspberries, and dandelion greens. We had fun but we also sustained our family's food needs this way as much as what we raised and grew.

One of our biggest recreational activities was hunting. All the men and boys, and many of the women-folk, hunted. This meant we needed to spend time cleaning and oiling our guns, and we needed to target practice.

I should point out two things here.

My beloved grandmother, Mamie, despised two things in life more than anything else.

Guns she hated even more than foul smells, and blood she feared, especially the sight of her own.

Heh, yeah, a picture is starting to develop, ain't it?

So, it was common to spend some time target shooting. With rifles meant for hunting of larger game, such as deer, we would load up the rifles and some paper targets and head to our gravel pit where we could set up a 100-yard range and dial those scopes in. It was considered sacrilegious to wound or miss a deer because the scope was not properly adjusted. One time my dad bought a semi-automatic 30.06 from some guy who was hard up for $100, and was proudly showing this gun off at the pit when we were target practicing. It was a great deal, $100 for a Remington .06 with a 3x9 Tasco scope was something to brag a little about. So, I ran down and set up a paper target on the side of the sand bank approximately 100 yards from where Dad's pick-up was setting crossways on the access road at the edge of the gravel pit, in the backfield of The Other Farm. I came back and noticed that Pup was still sitting in the passenger side of the pick-up. He said he wasn't shooting so there was no need to get out. He was just fine sipping his Narraganset beer and watching the action. Dad took off his coat and laid it across the hood of the truck, and standing on the driver's side of the truck he laid the rifle across the hood on his jacket, and squinted one eye as he peered through the scope. All went completely silent, sorta like when someone putts on the golf course. Then, a loud cracking KEEEE-Powwww split the silence.

Dad, had pulled the trigger.

I was watching the sand bank closely as it was my job to see the puff of dirt kick up on the sand bank to gauge how far off the scope was.

I didn't see a thing...nothing, and said so.

Dad growled, "You must have been daydreaming about girls. You mean to tell me you didn't see anything?"

"No sir, did you?"

"Nope, not in the scope, but you should have seen something on that sand bank."

I shook my head and held up my hands. Pup took another swig of beer and chuckled.

Dad, looking quizzical, picked up the gun to look at the scope, and when he did, his jacket slid off the hood of the truck, and there we both saw a hole punched through the hood. I looked it over and discerned that the bullet had gone through the hood of the truck, narrowly missing the passenger-side front tire and had buried itself in the sand on the side of the road.

This got Pup out of the truck.

"You boys let me know when you can hit that 150-foot tall and 300-foot wide sand bank with that gun. Till then, I think I'll stand behind you."

Yikes!

We did manage to get the ol' girl dialed in without further incident, and Pup decided it was safe enough to resume his position inside the truck. To the day Dad finally sold that pick-up, that bullet hole was ever present. He never fixed it. Probably as a reminder that one can never be too safe handling or shooting firearms.

On the other hand, we would target practice with our shotguns most anywhere, including the barnyard. Shotguns were used for hunting birds and other small game such as squirrel or rabbits, and the extermination of vermin such as rats or anything suspected of rabies. My family feared rabies more than anything else. So, it was critical to the war effort against rabies to be adept with the trusty ol' shotgun. We would randomly break them out and start shooting cans thrown in the air. Probably this happened when one of the men had a flash of rabies-fear and decided we all needed to have a crack at it, so to speak.

Every year in the late fall, three guys from New Jersey would come to Maine and stay with my grandparents to hunt birds and deer with Pup, Dad, and the uncles. Bill and Slim were about Pup's age and had met him while hunting with another Mainer a few years back. They struck up such a great friendship that the two of them stayed with Mamie and Pup on their hunting trips thereafter. A few years later, George, Bill's son-in-law, also started making the annual trek to Maine to spend two or three weeks with this farm family and to work and hunt with them. They loved it, and we loved them. They would always bring presents for the ladies and the kids, and they would privately ensure that Pup was "compensated" for his hospitality. Class acts.

One afternoon, Unc Stub and George decided they were going to take a ride up to the "mountain" to do a little bird hunting. It was the season for partridge, woodcock, and pheasant hunting. All three were fun to hunt. Walking through the old overgrown, long-since-active, apple orchards on the game preserve located on Frye Mountain, ten miles west of our farm, one would always flush a few and it was great fun to try your skill at shooting a bird in flight, not to mention the delicious bounty it provided for the next morning's breakfast table.

So, in preparation of this day's hunt, Stub and George decided a little target practice might be wise before heading out to the mountain. Pup was sitting on the cement steps of the shed attached to the house watching as first Stub would throw up a soup can or two and George would blast away at them. Then it was Stub's turn to shoot a few cans out of the air. The two of them had their backs to the house and were shooting in the air towards the woods beyond the chicken house. About as safe as it gets. Even for the chickens.

Timing, in life, is, as they say, everything. Stub threw an empty can of Campbell's tomato soup, with the opened lid bent back and hanging, in the air. George pulled the trigger on the 12 gauge shotgun, just as Mamie opened the shed door to holler that lunch was ready, to come and get it. George's shot was true, he hit the can, severing the hanging lid which went whistling through the air in an arc to come down and strike Mamie on the back of the hand as she stood in the doorway. She looked down and saw blood, her own blood.

"Oh my GOD Henry, I've been shot!"

Mamie almost fainted due to the sight of her blood, but it was really nothing more than a scratch. Pup and the boys managed to calm her down and once she realized what had happened, well, she did what she always did. She took her broom to the lot. Whack whack whack! Poor George figured he was gonna be banished to sleeping in the barn. After Mamie calmed down a bit, she even laughed about it. No one to that point even dared to crack a smile, so it was a big relief when she started laughing.

Later that day over dinner, Mamie giggled and told the story of the time when a partridge flew through the window of the shed, breaking the glass with such force it sounded like an explosion, and leaving the bird dead on the floor. Her elderly father was staying with Mamie and Pup at the time, and slept on a cot out in the shed. He came tearing into the house hollering, "Get down Selena! The Injuns are shooting at us!"

Good thing it wasn't true, Mamie would of wreaked havoc on those poor Indians with her broom, I'm sure.

Story Eight

Bull's Eye

On the farm, not only does each family member have chores and responsibilities to manage the farm properly, they feel an obligation to the community of neighboring farmers. It is quite common for neighboring farmers to accept a helping hand here and there as it may be needed, and to be ready to reciprocate that help when a neighbor needs it.

This helping hand may come in the form of helping with the haying, cleaning out the chicken barn, or helping with the building of a new barn. This sort of mutual back scratching is as old as farming itself and typically produces long-lasting friendships and even partnerships. It is a way for all farmers to save on expenses while maintaining more production, not to mention it allows for a bit of social gossip and pondering while getting those last 100 bales of hay in the mow before it rains.

At the same time, most farmers are quick to open their homes to visitors who may want to spend a week or so experiencing the life on a farm away from their lives in the city. We had such visitors when I was growing up. There were three men from New Jersey who would come up to Mamie and Pup's to spend a couple of weeks in November during the deer hunting season.

Pup was well known for his hunting abilities and befriended these hunters while they were up during a November hunt once, and from then on they would come and stay with us for their annual trek to Maine. Two of the three men, Bill and Slim, were friends who worked together back in New Jersey, and the third was Bill's son-in-law George, who was a police detective from Paramus, N.J.

It was always a treat for us kids when they came because they would bring lots of presents for us. I remember once getting a really cool cowboy toy pistol set and real cowboy hat from them.

The two weeks they would spend with us was filled with excitement. We would work extra hard to get the chores done so the men could hunt during the day, and at night around Mamie's table there would be the incredible stories and yarns of hunting adventures past. As the years passed and Bill and Slim got older, they didn't come as frequently and eventually both these gentlemen, who had become almost part of the family, passed away, but George and his wife, Eleanor, continued to come to Maine for two weeks in the summer and again for the two weeks in November.

The summer visits were always looked forward to, as Eleanor loved to spend time at the beach and would pry us kids away from the farm and take us to a local lake to swim and laze in the sun.

This story tells about how a series of events while helping out a neighbor farmer when we had visitors at our farm conspired to create what I termed "bull's eye".

On this particular day it was raining. It was in the summer, and George and Eleanor were up for their two week visit. Due to the inclement weather, haying was out of the question, so it was decided that it would be a good day to lend the bull out. One of the neighbor farmers had a cow which was ready to conceive and needed the services of a bull. Pup and Unc Gene happened to have such a bull. This bull had performed his duties with our own heifers vigorously, and seemed ready to take to his duties with anticipation for more.

So, Pup called the neighbor farmer, Ivory Young, mentioned to him that it might be a good day to bring his heifer down and let the two of them frolic in our pasture for a time. Ivory readily agreed and said he would load her on his truck and be along.

So, Pup, Unc Gene, Dad, Cousin Genie, me, and our visitor, George, decided we should round up the bull in the pasture and put him in the corral until the heifer showed up. It was a big pasture, and we didn't want to take any chance the bull wouldn't pick up the scent. We figured it would be "automatic" if the bull and the heifer were introduced, so to speak, inside the corral that was about 50 feet in diameter.

We traipsed out in the rain to the pasture and spread out in an ever closer circle until we drove the herd, with the bull, to the corral. Once the bull moved inside the corral, we shooed the rest of the herd off and closed the gate and waited for Ivory to show up. While we waited, George was wisecracking that he was at least smart enough to wear a rain outfit while the rest of us were soaking up the rain in our flannel shirts and caps. George was in fact outfitted in his bright yellow rain slicker and pants complete with the matching mariner's rain cap, all shiny with the rain, and he was completely dry.

We were soggy and getting soggier by the minute, but before long we saw Ivory putt-putting down the road in his 1954 GMC pickup with the high wooden sideboards, complete with heifer aboard. Genie ran over to the edge of the road and opened the gate in the fence and Ivory backed his truck in to the corral. Genie shut the gate and ran back over and we all took our positions.

The idea was to let the tailgate of the truck, which was about six feet high and acted as a ramp, down into the opening of the corral while at the same time not letting the bull out of the corral.

I did mention that the bull was highly interested in performing his duty didn't I?

Yes, by this time the bull was quite aware of the heifer's scent and was pacing all around the corral, grunting and getting all wide-eyed.

It was up to Genie and me to run interference on the bull and try to keep him from rushing the truck. The bull was not particularly happy with this arrangement and was bellowing and snorting at us. Meanwhile George and Dad were standing on one side of the truck, with Dad on the inside, closer to the truck while George was on the outside, closer to the corral. Pup and Unc

Gene were doing the same thing on the other side of the truck, as they pulled the pins and lowered the tailgate of the truck.

Ivory was inside the body of his truck with the heifer ready to convince her to back down the ramp/tailgate into the corral where her amour was waiting...impatiently.

You know, sometimes it's funny how things work out. The moon and stars all line up just so...

On any other given day, it could have been someone else standing there. Or, it could have been Dad that was standing on the outside instead of George. Perhaps it was that shiny yellow rain slicker. I'm not sure exactly why it happened, but it did.

Just as the tailgate was being lowered, the heifer got shy and refused to back up, the bull had decided he had waited long enough and rushed forward past Genie and me toward the heifer's scent. George was bent over at the waist just setting the tailgate onto the ground and the bull mounted him.

I mean mounted him.

Front legs and hooves hooked over his shoulders and he was, to coin an old army expression, locked and loaded.

George stood straight up, which I think just encouraged the bull, and then he turned into the corral and tried to run out from under the bull.

Personally, I would have never recommended that course of action...but no one asked me.

Anyway, George was trying to run with this bull mounted on his back doing what horny bulls are supposed to do, and he is screaming, "Get him off me...Get HIM OFF ME!!"

Pup, Unc Gene and Dad ran over and grabbed the bull, dragged him off George just as Ivory got the heifer into the corral.

The bull decided he better take another stab at it, so to speak, and went after the heifer, and in a matter of minutes they were busy with each other.

George, who by the way, was a police detective in Paramus, N.J., was standing there in complete and utter amazement, eyes wide, with the funniest look I've ever seen, on his face.

Damn sure wished I had a camera.

Pup, Unc Gene, Dad, Ivory, Genie, and I couldn't help ourselves. We were holding onto the corral to keep from falling down we were laughing so hard. Pup finally got himself under control and said, "Damn, George, I believe that bull has a thing for you."

George was still speechless, shaking his head and trying to figure out what had just happened. Unc Gene offers, "That's why the rest of us ain't wearing them fancy rain suits, damn bull will take to them every time."

Like I said, perhaps it was the shiny rain slicker, or maybe it was because George happened to be in the right position, I don't know. I do know that he and Eleanor continued to come to the farm for years after that, but I never once saw George wear a yellow rain slicker in the pasture again.

Story Nine

Morrill General Store

Here in Maine the general store is still, to this day, the de facto community center in some of the more rural areas and small towns. It certainly was in my grandfather's day. Morrill General Store was the quintessential village store that offered everything from "soup to nuts" plus a healthy dose of gossip, Red Sox discussions, and of course...weather reports. (Think "Drucker's Store" from the TV show "Green Acres" for those of you who remember that TV comedy based on life in a small farming community.) Weather reports were always the rage in any gathering when you lived and worked in a farming community, because so much depended upon the weather. It was always interesting to listen to the self-described weather gurus and their particular way of predicting what was to happen, weather-wise, and what had conspired yesterday that caused their weather report to be off just a tad. One time a local farmer insisted that even though the skies were cloudless and blue, and that those "idiots" on channel 5 up in Bangor said there would be nary a drop of rain for several days to come, that it would indeed rain later that day. He went on to explain that when his left elbow swelled up and he had trouble bending it without it hurting it was sure to rain--guaranteed. Never failed him in all his years of weather predicting. His brother, who worked their family farm with him, chuckled at this and reminded him, "Maynard, it might be that your elbow is all swelled up because you banged it wicked hard on the hay baler this morning yanking that piece of twine out of the gears."

As it happened, those "idiots" on channel 5 up in Bangor, got it right this particular time, it did not rain for several days.

No rain meant happy farmers, and one could drive around Waldo County on sunny summer days and see fields being mowed, or fields that had been mowed being raked into winnows or rows of loose hay, or fields full of winnow rows of hay being baled by a contraption hauled behind a tractor, called a baler, that ate the rows of winnowed hay and spit a bale of hay, neatly tied, out the other end. Once the hay was baled, it was then time to take the hay truck and/or hay wagons and drive around the field and pick up all those bales of hay and transport them to the barn to be packed into the hay mow for the farm animals' winter meals.

On rainy days, farmers likely spent the time repairing their farm equipment or working on the ever-present "honey-do" list their wives were always updating, or going to the store (pronounced "th' stowa") for supplies, groceries, grain, equipment parts, nails, gas, baling twine, fishing line, a new dung fork, bag balm, seeds for the garden, a new pair of gum rubber boots to replace the ones that had been patched so many times that it was impossible to patch them again, beer (very important), one of those new-fangled toasters for Mother's kitchen, or what have you. While the shopping was important, so was the social aspect of an hour or two at th' stowa.

One day in late July, when I was nine, it was a day that sloshed back and forth between rain and a heavy mist. That meant we couldn't hay, so Unc Gene, Pup, Cuz Genie-bub and I piled into the old '59 blue Ford pickup and headed to Morrill General Store for a couple of bags of grain and a few other supplies. Pup had a list from my grandmother as well for various cooking supplies that she wanted him to pick up for her.

"As long as you're going anyway," she said with a note of disappointment.

You see, Mamie went into town once a week on Saturday evenings to do her week's shopping in Belfast, where there were department stores as well as bona fide grocery stores. That's when she would socialize with other ladies who were shopping.

So, the four of us tool up the road to Morrill Village about six miles away, Unc Gene is driving, Pup is sitting by the door on the passenger side, and Genie-bub and I are wedged in the middle. When we get to the store, Unc Gene backs the truck up to the loading dock of the grain barn attached to the side of the store, between two other pickups whose owners are likewise loading grain onto the body of their trucks. One of the trucks belongs to a neighbor farmer by the name of Harry Copson. With Harry that day were two other fellas, one being his brother Bruce and some guy wearing a cowboy hat and honest to goodness cowboy boots--a novelty around these parts. Maine farmers wear Dickies, plaid shirts, suspenders, shitkickers, and ball caps with things like John Deere or Case on them. It was fairly easy to tell this fella wasn't from around here. We get out of the truck and Pup and Unc Gene nod to Harry and Bruce, and Pup says, "Shitty hay weather, eh?"

Harry and Bruce both nod back.

"Sure is, Henry...Hey, Gene..boys," says Harry by way of a greeting.

Harry, Bruce and cowboy boots all jump down from the body of their pickup and lean against the side of it, while we are leaning against the side of ours, and a conversation strikes up.

There is talk of the weather, then a bit about the ever-rising cost of baling twine and grain, "hard to make ends meet", when the next Grange meeting will be, and who the speaker is supposed to be, how the gardens are doing, etc.

Then Bruce introduces cowboy boots to us as Tom Bodine from Texas, a friend of his he met while serving in the Navy years back. Tom, a rancher back in Texas, was up for a visit and was getting a first-hand taste of farming in Maine. Handshakes all around and then Tom asks Pup, "So, Henry, how big is your spread?"

Pup gets that twinkle in his eyes and responds, "Spread?...well, on our farm we spread nothing but cowshit...but I've heard that Bruce likes to spread the other kind."

We all chuckle and Tom tries again, "No, I mean how big is your ranch...err...farm?"

Pup shrugs his shoulders and says, "Oh...dunno for sure...probably 300 acres or so...enough....all we can take care of."

Cowboy Tom sees his opening and drawls, "Well sheeit, I get up in the morning and get in my pickemup truck and drive all day, and I don't get to the other end of my spread."

Pup pats ol' Tom on the shoulder in a gesture of commiseration and shakes his head sadly, "Heyuh...used to have a truck like that once."

While cowboy Tom is blinking, and thinking that one over, we say our good-byes and Unc Gene and Genie-bub head into the grain shed while I follow Pup into the store to pick up the list of supplies. We go up one aisle and then down the next, grabbing the things on the list, then crossing those off the list with a pencil stub that Pup carries in his shirt pocket.

We are about halfway down one aisle and I am reaching for a bottle of cod liver oil (yuck, but hey...it was on the damn list) and I notice Pup is looking at someone coming up the aisle from the other direction. I look at a woman who is probably in her early 60s, blue haired, glasses perched at the very end of her nose, and she is consulting a list of her own. Pup, clearly, knew this woman because he says, "Well...hello Alice...how's your ass?"

Alice is clearly startled because she jumps back, looks at Pup, then looks at her list again, looks back our way, notices me, and snaps, "Shut up, Henry Littlefield!"

Pup deadpans, "Huh...so's mine...s'pose it's the weather?"

Alice took off in a huff. As I started snickering, Pup told me that I better hurry and finish the list before I got him in any more trouble. We managed to finish the shopping and get back out to the truck without any further incidents. This one still makes me chuckle whenever I think of it.

Story Ten

The Coincidence

My grandfather was a farmer all of his life…well, with the exception of the period of time that he was a "kept man" by a nurse in Boston, but that is another story for another time. Being a farmer is an interesting career. One has to be capable of figuring things out, from how to help a sheep who is breech give birth, to "what are we gonna do with all that cow manure?" As if that isn't enough, the farmer has to truly be a jack of all trades, which means he must spend his time wisely as there are always a hundred little chores one must get done. I remember one morning when I was about seven, my grandmother asking my grandfather the same question for four mornings in a row, "Henry, when are you going to fix the leak in the roof?"

On the first morning his answer was, "Well Mother, it ain't leaking today, it ain't raining."

The next morning, as it so happened, it was raining, "Can't fix it today Mother, it's raining."

The third morning brought a glare from my grandmother along with the same question, to which my grandfather responded, "Soon Mother. Gotta tend the hay laying in the lower field today. If'n I don't that rain we had yesterday will ruin it."

The fourth morning dawned bright and clear. It was going to be another beautiful Maine summer day. My grandmother was up extra early and lying in wait for my grandfather when he came out of the bathroom after his morning "constitutional". She demanded a definitive answer to the same question she had been asking for the last four days, "When are you going to fix the roof?"

Henry pondered a beat or two and replied, "The first."

"The first?" my grandmother questioned with a puzzled look on her face. "Henry, today IS the first...the first day of July." She began to look hopeful.

Pup shook his head sadly, "No, Mother, not the first of July, the first chance I get."

In these early morning exchanges between my grandparents, I began to see the importance of time management skills, as well as the art of negotiations.

Anyway, as a farmer, Pup always said that breakfast was the most important meal of the day. If a man was to work hard out in the fields all day, then he must start the day with a real meal. And he did. Henry's breakfast was typically a three-course meal that most folks would consider dinner or supper if you prefer. So, every morning starting about 4:30 a.m., Henry would begin to prepare breakfast for a table which usually consisted of me, my Dad, my Unc Stub, and himself. Sometimes we would be joined by another of my uncles, or whoever may have been working with my Dad and Unc Stub. It was always interesting watching my Dad and Unc try and come to life at 5:00 a.m., as they sat bleary-eyed over their cup of coffee and watched Pup whistle and dance around the kitchen preparing anything from pot roast, potatoes, gravy and biscuits, to venison steaks, eggs, fried potatoes, and biscuits.

One particular morning, a Sunday, Pup appeared to be especially happy, his whistling and dancing around the kitchen had a decided upbeat to it. Coincidentally, Dad and Unc Stub seemed even more bleary-eyed than usual. I figured it was because it was a Sunday, and Saturday night was, for those two, what we commonly referred to as a "large" evening. In fact, if you dared, you might even consider Dad and Unc to be a bit irritable that morning.

"Jeez, Father, you seem pretty damn happy this morning," says Unc Stub as he stared into his coffee cup.

"Well," says Pup, as he shuffled a pound or two of fried potatoes onto Unc's plate, "we had quite the coincidence here this morning."

Neither Unc nor Dad responded to that for a few minutes, instead opting to shovel down some food, but then Unc couldn't resist, "A coincidence?"

"Heyuh," Pup deadpanned. "Me, the old lady, AND the alarm clock all went off at the same time."

I figured that Pup must have found time to fix the leaky roof.

Story Eleven

Smoke Signals

In today's world we have become accustomed to "staying connected", from cell phones that take pictures and text messages, to Blackberrys that not only allow you to talk to whoever you would like anywhere any time, but access your email, get a stock market quote, go onto the internet, and even watch your TV at home while you are out and about. Amazing when you stop and think about it. Imagine, if you can, what it must have been like to experience that new-fangled contraption called the telephone back in the 1930s. Oh, I know, you history buffs will correct me and point out that telephone service was established before the 1930s, but it was still in its infancy out on the rural country roads and farms around Belfast, Maine. Even then, this new form of communication was met by many with varying degrees of suspicion.

Especially the farmers.

Idle chat was something saved for the weekly trips to the store in town, or the county fair in the fall of the year. Didn't seem right to be able to just pick up this funny-looking piece of black iron and stick in to your ear and talk to someone.

Now the farmers' wives loved it, they finally had a way to keep up with the local gossip and get the "skinny" before their neighbors did. Oh my, the juiciness of being able to get and give gossip so readily was just too enticing to pass up. Of course they told their husbands it was critically necessary to spend the money to have telephone service because it was a security measure in the event of fire or sickness, and would only be used in such emergencies, but in reality the telephone quickly became the biggest source of entertainment for many.

In those days, not only did every call have to go through an operator, who would come onto the line with "Operator, who may I connect you to?", but each telephone subscriber was one of six to eight members of a "party line". The party line meant that you shared that line with the other homes in the general area, and therefore had to share the time you could use the telephone. Unless, of course, one just wanted to chat with the members on that line, or listen in on their conversations to others, which many did.

Yes, eavesdropping or "telephone snooping" soon became a dirty little secret that many could not resist, but would never ever admit to. Telephone wars soon broke out between the party line members, "That old biddy, Erma Johnson, ties up the line all day. If we had a fire here, we'd burn flat to the ground before I could call the fire department. You should hear the things she tells people. Why, it's scandalous!".....or, "I tried to call down to the store to see if they had any roofing tar come in like you asked me, but Hazel Wilcox tied up the line for two hours straight! Did you know that she thinks Harry Potter is spending far too much time over to the Brown farm helping out poor Tom's widow? She says Harry's wife is not very pleased. Tch tch...can't say that I blame her," might be what a farmer would hear from his wife when he came into the house for supper after being out in the fields all day.

You can see why a lot of farmers had some trepidation about the telephone.

My grandfather's sister, Lilabelle, or Aunty Belle, as she was known to all of us, was married to a man by the name of Walter Cunningham. Walter was born with a cleft palette and therefore "talked funny". Walter was, due to his impediment, a man of few words and was also known for his short temper. Not long after Aunty Belle had convinced Walter that they needed to have telephone service installed, "for safety reasons mind you", Walter came into their house and announced that he needed to find out if a part he had ordered for the car had come in yet, and would Aunty use that damned telephone to call Ed at the garage and find out before he walked to town to get it. Aunty figured it was time that Walter learned to use the telephone himself in the event he ever needed to "for safety reasons mind you." So, she instructed him to call Ed himself, and told him how to do so. Walter looked at the phone warily but picked up the receiver, stuck it to his ear and heard the nasally "Operator, who may I connect you to?"

"I need to talk to Ed down to his garage in town," replied Walter in his even more nasally cleft palette speak. The operator told Walter that he must either give her this "Ed's" telephone number or his address so she could look it up and try to connect them, to which Walter responded, "It's the only damn garage in town."

Aunty Belle stepped in and told Walter the number to the garage and said, "Just tell her to connect you to this number Walter." Walter told the operator the number Aunty have given him, to which the Operator responded, "Sorry sir, that line is busy...please try again later."

So, Walter waited for 15 minutes or so and tried again. This time when he picked up the telephone and stuck the receiver to his ear he heard several female voices to which he queried, "Is this that operator?" He was ready with the number this time as Aunty had written it down for him. "No," came the response, "This is Shirley Bennett, Walter, we have the same party line as you and Belle. I'll be only a few more minutes and then you can make your call...try again in 15 minutes."

Walter's first telephone experience was not going well, and his famous short fuse was getting shorter by the second.

15 minutes later, Walter once again picked up the receiver, the operator comes onto the line, "Operator, who may I connect you to?" Walter once again gave her the number, and once again, as fate would have it, she responded, "Sorry sir, that number is busy, please try later." By this time, Walter has had all of this new telephone contraption he wants and in utter frustration

hollered at the operator, "You can take this telephone and shove it up your ass!" hung up and stomped out of the house.

Heh....wait, it gets even better.

The operator, a local Belfast girl was understandably upset at Walter's suggestion and immediately called her area supervisor and told him what happened. The supervisor, a fella by the name of Jim Thompson, promised her he would go speak to Walter about proper telephone etiquette. Belfast was a pretty small town, Jim and Walter knew each other fairly well, so when Jim walked up to the door of Walter and Aunty Belle's home and knocked, he was welcomed into the kitchen and asked if he'd like a cup of coffee. Jim accepted the coffee and told Walter why he had come to pay a visit.

"Walter, I know you got frustrated and didn't mean what you said, but you cannot speak that way to one of my operators. I'm afraid if you don't apologize to this operator, I am going to have to take your telephone away from you. Now, will you call the operator and speak to her?"

"Yes," Walter said, "I will."

Walter picked up the telephone and the operator comes onto the line, "Operator, who may I connect you to?"

"Is this the operator I told to take the telephone and shove it up her ass?"

"Yes, it is," came the icy reply.

"Well, get ready, 'cause he's bringing it right down."

This is one of my favorite stories about my family before I was around. Every time I heard it, I couldn't stop laughing long enough to find out if Aunty Belle and Walter ever got telephone service again.

Story Twelve

The Chicken Capital of the World

The sleepy little town I grew up in held this distinctive title for many years: The Chicken Capital of the World.

I was born during the height of the boomer generation, 1956. By that time Belfast had already enjoyed a long history of raising and processing poultry for not only the entire U S of A, but Canada as well. However, after World War II, as our nation got busy making babies at a prodigious rate, the chicken industry boomed to an all-time high that, naturally, coincided with the arrival of all us babies.

Belfast, and the surrounding towns of Waldo County, offered the ideal area to grow such a business. While Belfast proper had a blue collar populace, and the town boasted a variety of factories—shoe, pants, sash and blind, and a sardine processing plant—the chicken industry offered employment for not only the factory workers, but the entire county and beyond.

Yes, the chicken processing plants employed lots of people and the wages were usually better than what some of the other factories paid. They were unionized so the employees felt they had a sense of ownership in the plants and many of those employees worked at these processing plants their entire lives.

But, the raising of the birds employed many of the surrounding farmers in Waldo County and beyond. Most every farmer within 50 miles of the Belfast processing plants got in on the action. Raising chickens for the poultry plants offered the farmer an additional income stream which quickly became a main component of farming in Maine during the 20th century. So, during those (chicken) salad days, Belfast became the chicken capital of the world and processed, on average, 250,000 chickens a day.

That's a lot of soup.

But then it changed. By the early 1980s, Belfast's factories started dwindling. Over the next several years they all closed or relocated, with only Matthews Brothers remaining operational in its new location off the waterfront. Gone were the shoe factories, the sardine processing plant, the pants factories, and the largest employers in Waldo County, Maplewood and Penobscot Poultry Company.

By the mid-1980s, the chicken industry was all but dead in Maine, with Penobscot Poultry closing its doors on February 24, 1988. It was the end of a way of life. The combination of increased cost of doing business, stiffer government regulations, along with a growing desire by some of the newer residents of Belfast to perform what they called "the beautification of Belfast" by waterfront genocide to remove the ugly factories on "their" ocean front--all succeeded in driving the industry out of Maine and into the southern States.

The unemployment rate in Belfast in those days of the latter 1980s exploded to almost 20%.

They say it was all for the protection of the populace, due to unsafe working conditions in the factories, lack of benefits for the workers, and the spiraling cost of doing business, but that always made me scratch my head and wonder. I believed those factories and those people just didn't fit into the new plan for Belfast.

It is important to note that while the factories were ugly, and smelly, and were taking up residence on prime ocean frontage, they provided decent paying jobs to many people. Those people, those factory workers, while less educated and less "intellectual" than the new Belfastians, were tough, gritty, savvy, honest, hardworking, and reliable. They worked hard, and they played hard. They were loud and somewhat bawdy, but they also stood behind one another. They lived, worked, and raised families-- they were a community. They have left an undeniable legacy.

Why, back in the day when Belfast had its waterfront littered with two large chicken processing plants, two shoe factories, a pants factory, a potato processing plant, two sash and blind factories, a sardine/shrimp processing plant, several marine/boat yards, and the bay was filled with lobster and other fishing boats, the fishing was fantastic! The bay was wealthy with lobster, mackerel, striped bass, blue fish, dog fish, crabs, and clams.

There was NO unemployment.

This little town of 6,000 boasted four hardware stores, at least four banks, an upper and lower five and dime, a variety of pubs, diners, and restaurants, several menswear shops, many ladies apparel shops, beauty salons, magazine shops, five bakeries.

You get the picture.

A blue collar town...blue collar mentality...

Oh, there were a few "elite", your bankers, your lawyers, your doctors and your dentists, etc., but even the factory owners, who likely were the wealthiest in town, were considered blue collar. There were no empty storefronts in Belfast, there was no need to go to Bangor shopping because everything we needed could be found right here in this sleepy little chicken-feather-laced community.

So anyway, before the many changes that occurred in the mid-70s through the mid-80s, or what we generational families refer to as "back in the day", each summer the city would honor its title of chicken capital of the world by hosting a festival. "The Broiler Festival" soon became known as the highlight of the summer for Belfast and surrounding cities and towns. The city would certainly get a boost in the economy as thousands would come to town to partake in the carnival-like festivities. The festival itself was held at the Belfast City Park, a beautiful 20-acre park on the ocean just south of the middle of town.

It, to this day, is still one of the few city parks located on the ocean on the east coast of America. The week-long festival took place in the middle of July and boasted a parade (there HAS to be a parade), a huge chicken barbecue held on the tree and dandelion-dotted grassy lawns of the city park, and a Broiler Queen contest.

Keep in mind, many of the events and the BBQ itself were staffed by citizen volunteers, my own dad q'd many a chicken over those hot coals for a few years running.

There WAS a carnival, too. The city park would fill with breathtaking carnival rides, games of challenge, booths filled with trinkets and stuffed animals, incredible shows of magic and mystery, food stands that made one's belly growl, and other exotic neon-laced enticements.

Tents were set up to host speakers who addressed political and social concerns, and to give local musical artists a venue in which to perform. There were boxing matches, and arm wrestling, and hot-rod shows. The smell of hot dogs, pizza, sausage and onions, dough boys, cotton candy, and greasy French fries wafted through the warm July nights, while our eyes were gleefully assaulted by the flashing neon lights and our eardrums joyfully brutalized by the blaring music of the seemingly hundreds of oversized speakers scattered throughout the midway. This carnival would start on Monday and run through Saturday when the festival ended with the BBQ. The rides and booths would usually open around noon and run til the wee hours. All the while this was going on, there were other events too. 4H events, speakers reporting on how legislation was working for the farmer and for the factory worker, bingo under a big top, educational and artistic groups, shiny new John Deere tractors featuring all the new and latest bells and whistles. All these events competed with the carnival for an audience.

The one event that would draw everyone's attention from the barkers, the balloons, and the neon, was the beauty pageant.

The Broiler Queen Pageant was always highly anticipated, hugely advertised, wonderfully coordinated, and genuinely the "crowning" event of the entire festival. Young women from all over the county would participate, and the city's business owners would be quick to help sponsor these ladies in hopes of riding the eventual Queen's tiara to business marketing heaven. Now, when the Queen was chosen, the family members of the new Queen, of course, enjoyed bragging rights for an entire year.

I imagine the pride my father felt the summer of 1967, as he was grilling chicken over hot coals, side by side with other men from the community that Saturday after the parade, for the huge BBQ that marked the end of another week-long festival, knowing it was his own daughter that was riding on the back seat ledge of a brand-spanking new Chevy convertible, in the parade that preceded the BBQ, looking so beautiful in her gown and the Queen's tiara.

When my sister Debbie, was crowned "Queen Chicken", my entire family glowed with pride and excitement. Mom and Dad were so happy they were actually nice to each other. All the uncles and aunts were waiting in line to hug and congratulate Sis, and as she was the first of her generation. I know our grandparents, Mamie and Pup, were especially proud of their brood. It was quite a celebration for our family.

Heh...I knew that I intended to use my newfound fame for as long and for as much as I could get out of it.

Hey, being the little brother to the ranking Broiler Queen had some benefits.

Well now, to get to this point, to be able to have a Broiler Festival, there had to be the chickens. Raising the chickens for the processing plants was something my family was very involved in. From the beginnings of the fledgling industry in the mid-1940s, to its demise the latter 1970s, we Littlefields were involved. Some of us even worked in the processing plants, which I will describe later, but let's go back to the beginning, where it all started.

The chicken industry in Waldo County went beyond the two largest and most recognized processing plants, Maplewood and Penobscot. In fact, before it became known as a potato processing plant, Penobscot Frozen Foods also bagged and froze processed chickens from the chicken processing plants, and offered meat lockers for people to store the family's supply of meat. My dad worked for Ted Starrett at Penobscot Frozen Foods for some time, and in fact, helped develop what we know now as packaged pre-cut chicken. By identifying the precise places to cut the chicken's legs and wings in the joints that make the legs and wings on a chicken work, they discovered the chickens could be packaged as a whole cut up chicken, yet be uniform and presentable to the buying public. These chickens called "fryers" or "broilers", were smaller and the growing cycle for the chicken farmer was shorter. Chickens that were raised to be fryers/broilers were typically raised in an eight to ten-week cycle. Larger birds, roasters or capons, were raised in longer cycles, 12-15 weeks. Not all fryers/broilers were cut up, at least initially. Most were marketed and sold whole, but the chickens that were slightly flawed in some way were cut up and sold as whole chickens—pre-cut, or, as packages of wings, legs, breast etc.

Now-a-days, consumers demand more cut-up chicken than whole birds, so the equation has changed from what it was in those days. As we became a society that wanted more convenience in our daily lives, we didn't want the pedestrian duty of cutting up our own chickens to feed our family, therefore the amount of whole birds marketed in relation to chicken parts that are packaged and sold has flip-flopped. To say that process of cutting up chickens that Dad and the folks at Penobscot Frozen Foods help develop for the processing plants was revolutionary might be a bit of an overstatement, but in fact, it did change how chickens were marketed.

Also, it is important to note that other farmers raised egg laying hens. These birds produced millions of eggs for market. The birds were in the same barn as long as they produced eggs--sometimes two to three years. Imagine what it was like to clean those barns! The chickens in those barns were typically kept in wire cages and the daily dung fell onto the floor of the barns, which was then shoveled through scuttle holes to the basement below. Then a tractor with a bucket would scoop the poop, so to speak, and load it onto a truck to be hauled off to the ever-growing pile of chicken shit at the far edge of one of the farm's fields. One could always identify a farm that had egg-layers, because the barns were one-story affairs. I would also point out, where there were chickens of any kind being raised or housed, there was grain to feed them.

Where there is grain, there are rats.

Very big rats.

Rats, evidently, thrive on grain.

The typical farmer usually had two defenses against the rats, a dog, and his sons. The dogs took pride in their defense of the chickens, and the sons loved the chance to target practice with the .22s that most every farm boy got for Christmas around his 10th birthday. This function was especially important when the chickens were little peepers, because they had no chance against the rats.

Rats like chickens, too.

So anyway, Penobscot Frozen Foods, Penobscot Poultry, and Maplewood Poultry were not the only pioneers of the chicken industry in Waldo County. So were Berry Brothers, or as they became known, Berry Bro's. Not only did Owen and Irvin Berry own and operate a chicken processing plant in Morrill, Maine, that employed over 100 people, but they owned several farms that raised the birds they processed. This was unique because the other processing plants, Maplewood and Penobscot, by and large, contracted with farmers to raise the birds they processed, whereas Berry Bro's, who did contract with local farmers to a small degree, owned and operated their own farms where most of the birds they processed came from. One such farm was referred to as "The Plantation".

The Plantation was located in Searsmont, Maine, and raised several hundred thousand chickens at a time. The revolutionary design of the "Quonset" style chicken house was developed there and became the new trend in chicken houses everywhere that chickens were raised. My grandfather, my father, and two of my uncles, harvested timber from our family's woodlots, sawed and milled the trees into the lumber used to build these new-fangled chicken houses. They also worked for Berry Bro's building and maintaining those chicken houses on the Plantation. My great uncle Lyle was the night watchman on the Plantation and spent most of his time every night shooting predators trying to get a warm meal.

No, not people...animals, chicken hawks, rats...Unc didn't shoot any people. Folks back then didn't steal chickens.

Didn't have to.

If they were hungry and needed a chicken or two to feed their family, no farmer would turn them down.

Ok, how are we doing so far? Lot to this chicken business eh?

Moving right along, feeding and watering the chickens, of course, was the biggest daily chore the farmer had. Chickens were fed grain. In the early days most chicken houses had a large shed attached to the barn that held the grain, commonly referred to as the "grain room". The grain room also was used to store extra feeders and waterers, as well as extra stoves used to heat the houses, and the fuel supplies that the stoves needed to function. Back in those days most chicken houses were heated with coal-fired stoves, but some used propane, while others used oil. My family, at one time or another, used all three of these types of stoves.

The grain came by truck in 100-lb bags, off-loaded into both floors of the grain room, then from there lugged to each of the three floors that housed the chickens each time they were fed...which was early morning and late afternoon. When the newborn chicks were delivered to the houses in cardboard crates, we dumped them lovingly inside an 18" high cardboard barrier set up around each stove in an appropriate 12-foot diameter. Each stove sported a large sheet metal bonnet sitting on it that looked like an umbrella, all of which created a safe and warm environment for the newborn chicks. The floor had been covered with fresh sawdust, and we used cardboard trays placed inside the barriers to put the grain "mash" in for the little chicks to eat. The water they drank was in gallon glass or plastic jugs that were threaded at the mouth and had plastic covers with a ring or trough that allowed the water to self-feed when the jug was turned upside down and setting on the cover. As the chickens grew from little fuzzy yellow peepers into gangly clumsy adolescent birds that became large enough to roam the entire floor, the containing cardboard rings, the cardboard feeder trays, and the water jugs were removed and replaced with heavy gauge aluminum feeders that sat on the floor, and three-foot long self feeding water troughs that hung inches off the floor on chains.

In case you're wondering, on average there were 1 1/2 birds per square foot.

That's a lot of dust...and dung.

Later in the evolution of the chicken industry "bulk grain" came to be. This offered the farmer a huge break in the labor of feeding these creatures. Instead of 100-lb bags of grain to be toted to each floor from the grain room, bulk grain was blown in from trucks to large storage bins in the top floor or attic of each barn. These bins would gravity feed the grain into chutes that ran from the bottom of the storage bins down through each floor. Now, the farmer just walked up to the chute, stuck his five-gallon cohog pail under the dispenser, pulled the little trap door, and Voila!...grain would fill the pail. Almost like a garden hose, one could turn on/off the flow of grain easily.

Yes, this made the workload a little easier for the farmer, but make no mistake about it...raising chickens was tedious, dusty, ammonia-filled, grueling, work.

When you consider the fact that my family raised over 60,000 chickens at a time on two of the three operating farms we maintained, plus the responsibilities of raising over 400 head of sheep that needed shearing every year, 40 head of cattle, at times a dozen or so milk cows (milked by hand), assorted pigs, goats, ducks, horses and a donkey, AND approximately 8-10 acres of produce-bearing gardens to maintain, over 100 cord of firewood yearly that had to be harvested, haying, spreading manure, maintaining miles of fences, etc., you can see that farming was not for the faint of heart, or, for the lazy.

So, making the feeding of the chickens a little less labor intensive by the advent of bulk grain was appreciated, but taken with a "grain" of salt to most farmers.

It's all relative, there was always plenty of other stuff to do.

The daily grind of maintaining 60,000 birds in three barns on two farms along with all the other responsibilities of our farms was daunting, but became so ingrained that we thought of this as part of the ritual of farming.

Though the road I lived on was named Pitcher Road, it was locally known as "the Littlefield Road", because everyone living on that road was related. Growing up in this large extended family of aunts, uncles, cousins, parents and grandparents all of us relatives had a support system of people who played together and worked together.

As a boy I found plenty of time for play, adventure, and many cases, mischief, either alone or with groups of the neighbor kids/relatives, but I, along with all the members of the farm family, had responsibilities to the farms. Everyone pitched in together for work, even us kids. One of those occasions was when we prepared for the new chickens' arrival to one or more of the three chicken houses.

As I've mentioned, raising chickens was generally dusty, dirty, and very odoriferous hard work. Over seven thousand chickens lived together on each floor of the chicken house. At my grandfather's farm, the grain room was attached to the Quonset-style barn and held those 100-pound burlap bags piled on top of each other filled with, at first, baby chick mash for the baby chicks, and then a few weeks later, poultry feed for the now adult chickens. Bags of cracked corn and crushed stone lined the wall for the older chickens. Cracked corn was spread by hand in the final two weeks of the growing cycle to fatten up the broilers before being taken back to the factory. Crushed stone was also spread by the handfuls to help the chicken's digestion process. The stone in the bird's crop helped to grind up the food before digesting it to the stomach below. Below the grain room was the coal room that stored the fuel for the numerous stoves spread throughout each floor of the barn.

The men, my grandfather, my uncles, sometimes my dad, and we boys fed, watered, and cared for this huge flock daily. We didn't have automated feeders and waterers in those days. All the work was done by hand, once in the morning, and again in the late afternoon. This work consisted in part of carrying buckets of grain from the grain room to each feeder, up and down the stairs, in and out numerous times. Glass waterers were re-filled each day, and stoves were filled with coal twice a day to keep the young chicks warm and cozy. This work continued for seven to nine weeks for the pullets or broilers, and up to 14 weeks for the roasters. After a few weeks old, a crew of men from the chicken factory would come, herd the flock into a smaller fenced off section of each floor, and de-beak them by burning the tip of the top beak back. As a child I thought the purpose of that process was to keep them from pecking us, more especially, me, but in fact it was actually done to keep them from pecking each other. Chickens feel no loyalty toward each other and will very quickly turn on a weaker brother or sister and peck it to death. At nine weeks, the factory crew would return and again fence off the chickens to gather up the pullets to take to the factory. A long flatbed truck stacked several layers high with wooden crates would pull into the yard and up to the end of the chicken house. After loading all the pullets, the truck with each crate stuffed to the gills with chickens would slowly pull out of the yard. We'd stand in the driveway watching the feathers fly and listening to the squawking until it was out of sight down the road. A few weeks later the whole process would be repeated with the roasters.

Then it was time for the barns to be cleaned so the cycle could repeat itself. The raising of chickens was mostly done by the men and us boys, but the task of cleaning all that chicken dung often required the assistance of neighborhood boys and in many cases, neighboring farmers, who would expect the same in return when they cleaned their barns. A sort of very stinky, ammonia, dusty, laborious, mutual back scratching.

After the chicken house was cleared out of its inhabitants, this crew of men and boys descended on the barn intent on getting the task at hand done as quickly as possible. Not only was this perhaps the worst job to be done on the farm, but much like many things in the business world, time is money. The quicker the barn was ready for a new batch of peepers, the sooner that stipend starting trickling in.

Starting with the top floor we would shovel the packed chicken dung, mixed with old nasty sawdust, often times more than a foot thick, into wheelbarrows and dump this cocktail down three-foot square holes that were aligned with the same size holes on the second floor into dump trucks parked on the bottom floor. When the third floor was cleaned down to the cement, the crew would move to the second floor and clean it. The bottom floor was easier to clean because tractors with buckets could drive in to gather up the waste. On the other hand, the bottom floor usually had much more to deal with. I can tell you, on a hot July day, this work could be described in many ways--"fun" was not one of the words used. However, we did have fun, at times. The work was grueling, so we would take a 10-15 minute break every couple of hours. The men would usually drink a Narragansett while we boys would relish a cold root beer. Sometimes, we'd allow ourselves two! Hey, the first bottle was to knock down the clotted dust in our throats, the second one you could actually taste and enjoy. During these breaks there would be stories. Stories of chicken house cleanings of the past, hunting adventures, fishing yarns, general men-gossip, and such. It was always fascinating to me to let my mind run wild while hearing these stories told by my elders. Even as miserable as the work of cleaning the barns was, my grandfather and uncles would keep us smiling as we worked by singing dirty little ditties and reciting ribald stories that would also kick my fertile imagination into high gear.

So, you, the reader may be asking, "What did you do with all this chicken shit?"

Good question.

Well, Emma, our truck with a dump body, was responsible for hauling away most of the stuff. Sometimes a neighboring farmer would bring his truck along to help with that process. This dung had some value. It was used to fertilize hay fields and gardens. Chicken dung has a very high degree of nitrogen in it, meaning it is "hot". It was great for a quick start of the growing cycle for timothy and clover in the fields, and for many of the vegetables we grew in our gardens. So, the full trucks would haul the dung the three miles to one of our other farms, which coincidentally we had entitled "The Other Farm". There, a section of one of the fields was used to store this dung in huge piles for future use. It also kept the smell away from our houses. The chicken house was smelly enough on ordinary days, but stirring up that mess spread that ammonia chicken smell far distances.

Washing the dishes was considered woman's work in my family, and that rule spread to the chicken barn as well. While the men were cleaning the barn, the ladies had the task of cleaning the waterers. The two-piece glass waterers had caked on crud from living with the chickens for weeks, and getting them clean for the next round of baby chicks was not an easy task. They would set up two large metal tubs in the grain room, one for soapy water and one for rinsing, changing the nasty water every half-hour. Taking turns washing, rinsing, and stacking the clean waterers on long boards stacked four deep and four wide, the washing would take about three days to complete, but the camaraderie of story-telling, gossiping, and jokes would make the time fly by. When my sister and I were young, Mamie, Aunt Wilda, and Aunt Bev were the chief bottle washers, but as the next generation of girls grew old enough, Sis and her same-aged cousins took over the responsibility. Cousins Brenda, Rhonda, and Linda and Sis all share great memories of working on the waterers for several years. Rhonda remembers the time Mamie picked up a dirty waterer and found a nest of baby mice in it. Not fazed, she quickly disposed of the vermin and continued with the task at hand. When finished with the washing and cleaning up the grain room, Pup would give each of the girls a silver dollar for their efforts.

Huh, us boys got a few root beers.

Next came the sawdust truck which had a long chute attached to the back of it that would be shoved into the barn windows, and sawdust was blown into huge piles on both ends of each floor. I loved the day that the sawdust truck came, because we kids would get to play in the huge sawdust mounds, sliding down the sides and playing king of the mountain. Pup and the Uncs figured while we "yowins" (a term loosely translated that means "young'uns") were having our fun, the sawdust piles were being spread to some degree, so it was a win-win.

After we yowins had worn ourselves out, it was time to get to work spreading the sawdust about six inches deep over the floors. Using wheelbarrows and shovels we kids (boys and girls) worked together with the men to finish this chore. In the wintertime we would keep the coal stoves burning, and the warm and sweet-smelling barn was a cozy place to be. The next step to ready the barn for the new chicks was to place rolled corrugated cardboard rings around each coal stove. We'd tuck the bottom of the rings into the sawdust and edge it with our feet so it would be stable. Then we'd lay newspapers inside of these rings, so that the baby chicks wouldn't eat the sawdust. We kids had contests to see how fast we could lay papers, but Pup's inspection always made us be careful to lay them correctly with no sawdust showing. Next we filled the waterers and feeders and placed five of them in each circle. Now the chicken house was ready, and excitement mounted for us kids.

One of my favorite memories is when the day-old babies arrived. My cousins, Sis, and I would wait on the big rock on the front lawn guessing which upcoming vehicle sound would be the chicken truck, anxiety growing with each passing vehicle. When it did arrive, we kids would run to meet the small crew bringing this precious cargo. The covered trailer held stacks on stacks of cardboard boxes with circular breathing holes showing little beaks and fluffy heads peering out. Instead of the squawking of the grown chickens going to the factory, the greeting of soft peepers coming to us from the factory was music to our ears.

A little yellow puff of sweetness.

For many of us, this represented the better part of the life cycle.

Each of us would wait in line to carry a box of baby chicks into the barn and stack them in the grain room for the two upper floors and the coal room for the bottom floor. After the truck was emptied and on its way, we would take each box to a warm coal-fired stove circled with cardboard rings and papered so neatly. Then we would reach our hands into one of the four compartments in the box and lift out the soft little balls of fur, so warm and sweet. The memory of that act is still so vivid in my mind. Over and over we would reach in and gently empty out box after box of the babies into their new home. Then when we were finished, we would usually sit on the backside of shovels leaned against the wall of the barn, and take it all in while we enjoyed another rootbeer. For the ladies, their work in the barns was done until next time. For us boys it meant we had the highly anticipated period of "protecting these little chicks".

Yes, remember the rats?

Those rats loved baby chicks.

So, we boys who were old enough, would camp out at strategic spots within the barns with bee bee guns and .22s.

Heh, it made all the shit-shoveling worth it.

Of course we then would spin our own yarns of how many rats we managed to exterminate, but the truth was, Pup's dog, Lassie, was the king rat-killer.

Each year the poultry company would give bonus checks to farm raisers who raised the healthiest chickens with the fewest death rates. Pup and Unc Gene always received a bonus check, and a few times they enjoyed the coveted title of "Grower of the Year" by the poultry company. During those years they would be invited to a celebration and banquet hosted by Penobscot or Maplewood Company.

As you can see, raising chickens on our farms was perpetual work for the entire family. It was this family participation in the three farms my family owned and operated that became the foundation of this family. It has defined us, and these memories continue to do so to this very day.

Looking back, those days seemed simple, easy, and always fun-filled, but it was also the hard grueling work for the entire family that I have described. The ability of our grandparents to be the glue, to keep this boisterous family tight-knit, working and playing together, is something this family continues to celebrate. It is important to note that these stories contained within, have involved most of the family members. They have contributed with their memories and perspective, and without them, these stories would not be as rich and as colorful. To memorialize our grandparents, this family, and this way of life, is truly an honor for me.

Story Thirteen

A Difference of Opinion

This is a story about my youngest uncle, Gary, or "Stubby" as he was nicknamed. When people ask him how he got such a nickname he tends to imply that it has something to do with a certain part of his anatomy, but in fact he got the name from my grandmother's brother-in-law Spike, whose real name was Vernon.

Evidently, as the story goes, little Gary was so short when he reached the age of four he could run under the kitchen table without hitting his head and presto! He became "Stubby", later shortened to "Stub", and still carries that moniker to this day. Funny thing is... he isn't short at all.

Anyway, Unc Stub, as I said, is the youngest of his generation. He has three older brothers, Unc Gene, Warren (my Dad), and Unc Mo. He also has an older sister, Aunty Bev. There are 19 years between Unc Gene the oldest, and Unc Stub the youngest. Being the youngest, especially a mid-life baby has its advantages, but on the other hand, as Unc Stub likes to point out, his parents were highly experienced to all the tricks of the trade of being a teenager by the time it was his turn to take a shot at being the family rebel.

He managed.

Of course he probably figured he had big shoes to fill with the history of three brothers before him honing the ways of mischief.

There was the time that Unc Gene, the oldest, and my Dad, Warren, the next oldest, curled my Unc Mo, their five-year-old little brother, into the inside of a big ole truck tire, and pushed the tire down over a steep hill. Evidently the tire, with Unc Mo curled inside it, was still gaining speed when it fetched up rather quickly against a tree about half-way down the hill. Evidently, Unc Mo was not seriously hurt, but did lose his lunch, so to speak, and Unc Gene and Dad got a whacking from Mamie with the wooden yardstick she kept tucked in between the telephone stand and the wall.

Another time when Unc Mo was about the same age, his two older brothers decided it was time for him to learn to ride a bike, an old hand-me-down that Unc Gene first had, then Dad, now it was time to pass the torch once again. They decided to put Unc Mo on the bike and push it down the hill.

Recognizing a pattern here?

So, Unc Mo is on this bike which is once again gaining speed as it hurtled downhill. Dad said he was doing good too…real good…until the road curved. Evidently they had forgotten to show Unc Mo how to steer the bike, because he went off the road and hit a tree. Might have been the same tree, I don't know. He did, however, manage to get a "certain part of his anatomy" pinched between the seat of the bike he was riding and the tree that he hit.

Perhaps Unc Mo should have been the one who was nicknamed "Stubby".

Unc Gene and Dad suffered the yardstick again, and I think that was when Mamie decided that Unc Mo should be the one to go off to college for an education. Probably saved his life.

Anyway, Unc Stub had some brotherly history to overcome.

As older teenagers are sometimes known to do, Unc Stub decided that he and a couple of his friends should have a cocktail or two one evening, and thought they ought to try some of Pups homemade hard apple cider that he kept in two 50-gallon wooden barrels in his cellar. So Unc Stub took it upon himself to draw off a gallon milk jug full of the stuff, and sneak it out of the cellar. He met up with his two buddies and they proceeded to find themselves a spot off the beaten path to sit and talk, listen to the radio, and drink a little cider. They must have got into a great discussion, because it was along towards midnight before

Unc Stub finally came into the house doing the ol' cider shuffle—you know, that's where one takes a step forward, and then staggers back two steps, then repeats—all under the glare of my Grandmother. Unc Stub managed to maneuver himself to the stairs and up to bed with my Grandmother right on his tail doing that "tch tch tch" noise that she always did when she was not impressed with the behavior of one of her brood. Once in bed, Unc Stub decided perhaps he should spend a little time in the bathroom, as his stomach had decided that the cider he had drunk was no longer welcome. So, he got into the bathroom and hollers down the toilet in that unknown but very "guttural" language that we all have practiced at one time or another, until he was done and decided to rest awhile on the floor. Mamie is, to say the least, quite unimpressed, and even a little worried. She hollers down the stairs for Pup, waking him up, where she insists he come up to the bathroom toot-suite.

"Henry, he is so sick, if we don't do something, I'm sure he is going to die," Mamie pleads.

Pups assured Mamie with a grunted, "Let him die" and clumps back down the stairs to bed.

Unc Stub finally settled down and went to sleep, on the bathroom floor; Mamie goes back to her bed and does the same.

Did I mention this was a school night?

Yes, great planning on Unc Stub's part.

My grandfather hated to be the family alarm clock. He would call to you once, and if you did not get up, he would quietly walk up to your bedside and toss a glass of cold water on your face. Amazing how well that works.

Unc Stub was fully aware of that fact, so the next morning at 5:00 a.m. when Pup hollered up the stairs, he knew he better get his ass out of bed, or off the floor, as it were. Evidently, Unc Stub was having trouble with his tongue, as it was glued to the roof of his mouth; his head was throbbing, and his stomach churning.

Oh, yes….he had it good.

So, he thumped down over the stairs in just his underwear, walked past Pup sitting at the kitchen table reading the morning paper, and went over to the sink where he proceeded to down one glass of water after another, until he drank four full glasses, wiped his mouth with the back of his hand, never uttered a word, and stomped back up the stairs to his bedroom.

Mamie was taking this all in, standing in the doorway between the kitchen and the living room, in her housedress, with her glasses perched at the very end of her nose. She shook her head and made that tch tch tch noise again. She said, "Henry, I think you better have a talk with that boy, I believe he was out drinking last night."

Pup glanced up from his morning paper and remarked, "Well, Mother, the way that boy is drinking this morning, I don't think he's had a thing to drink in the last week."

Unc Stub managed to get himself ready for school, he somehow managed to eat and keep down the glob of glue called oatmeal that Pup served him for breakfast, and then Pup asked Unc Stub if he could come out to the barn for just a minute before he left for school.

In the barn, at 6:00 a.m., with a major league hangover, Unc Stub learned a very valuable lesson that morning. He and Pup had a nice conversation, one where Pup talked, Unc Stub listened. Pup didn't say an awful lot about the fact that he drank, got drunk, and then got sick. He didn't say too much about the fact that it was on a school night either. Pup probably figured he didn't have to. He did impress upon Unc Stub that the barn, the very one they were standing in, was for animals and drunks, if Unc Stub should decide to come home in that condition again, he was welcome to find a nice comfortable spot in the hay mow to sleep. Unc Stub agreed to those terms.

Unc Stub says he never had to sleep in the barn, but he says that Pup would every so often.

Story Fourteen

A Fine Kettle of Fish

While life on the farm seemed an endless adventure for a young fella with an over-active imagination, yours truly decided that he needed to expand his horizons, as it were, and look beyond the farm for cultural and educational experiences. Or, as my father put it, "You're old enough to start making some money towards your support, get a job that pays you."

Evidently, it was decided the critical work I was responsible for on the farm could be absorbed by the Uncs and Pup, so I could make enough money over the summer school vacation to buy my own school clothes.

So, at the tender age of 12, I, along with a large number of kids in my school, got up at the crack of dawn, packed a pile of sandwiches, filled rinsed-out milk jugs with water, and caught a ride with our dads to the meeting spot where a school bus would pick us up, transport us to various fields throughout Waldo County where we spent the last 3-4 weeks of our precious summer vacation raking blueberries.

How'd you like to be the babysitter, ahem, I mean...foreman... of one of those crews?

We actually did work. Most kids came from blue collar families and had a strong work ethic ingrained, but we also raised a lot of hell, snuck off in the bushes to smoke black market cigarettes (stolen from one mom/dad or another), tell outrageous lies, and skinny dip if there happened to be a farm pond nearby.

Fortunately for the beleaguered foreman who was charged with keeping us all alive and relatively unharmed while he tried to convince us to rake more, play less, there were usually a few adults along to make a few extra bucks, and to help keep us kids in line. I remember coming home one Friday afternoon after a week's work of raking berries, and Dad asking me over supper that evening what I made for the week. I showed him my paycheck, $28.09. He looked at the paycheck, and then he looked at me, he said, "I have next Monday off from work. I'm going with you to rake blueberries. You may want to get some rest Sunday."

The look on his face told me the story, I was able to easily connect the dots...Dad was not impressed with my week's paycheck. I knew next Monday was going to be a backbreaking day, or as my Dad who was so good with words put it, "Better a sore back, than a sore ass."

Good point.

Monday dawned bright and sunny. Dad and I were up before sunrise, packed a pile of peanut butter and jelly sandwiches, filled a couple of thermoses with iced tea, and headed for Crosby High School, where we met the school bus to be transported to Northport for the day's work. Dad was in a good mood and laughed and joked with the foreman, Dick Marden, on the bumpy ride on the back roads of Northport. There were a few other parents along with their kids to help out for the day. The overall mood was light and the bus buzzed with chatter and laughter.

Dad had issued me a challenge that morning on the way to Crosby. If I worked beside him, kept up with his pace, and only took a break when he did (he didn't take breaks, except for a quick sandwich and drink when coming back from the winnower, and lunch—20 minutes), then he would give his earnings that day to me. I knew this was a challenge I had no choice but accept. I also knew I was going to work hard that day. I figured this was one of those defining moments between father and son, and I decided that I wanted to out-rake my dad. I wanted to prove that I could work as hard as he always did.

I came close.

He out-raked me that day, but I know he was proud of my efforts and he was happy to tell Dick to put his earnings for that day on my paycheck at the end of the week. Together, we made over $100.00 that day—a veritable fortune in 1968. I was proud of the fact, later that fall, that I was able to buy all my clothes and supplies for school out of my three weeks of earnings raking blueberries that year, and still have money left over in my savings account.

Over the next two or three years this cycle repeated itself. I would help out on the farm with the Uncs and Pup through July when the need for extra labor was in high demand, i.e. shearing sheep, haying, maintaining the huge produce-bearing gardens, etc., and then raking blueberries in August to earn enough to buy my school clothes.

When I turned 15 in July 1971, the youngest age one could obtain a work permit to work for a legitimate non-farming business, I was hired by Stinson Canning Company to work for the remaining five weeks of summer school vacation.

Three salient points you the reader should be aware of before proceeding with this story.

One, Stinson Canning Company was a processing plant for sardines and for shrimp. Very fishy.

Two, my youngest uncle, Stub, was the foreman, and who I reported to. He believed in "reverse" nepotism.

Three, my beloved Mamie (my paternal grandmother), with whom I lived, had a nose like a bloodhound.

I should probably note here that I actually didn't work on the farm at all that summer. I was traveling the country with my sister and her husband. We had an incredible adventure that summer taking in such sights as Niagara Falls, and other notable tourist sites as we meandered west, first to Kansas where her husband, Steve's, family lived, to finally end up in Colorado where they spent the next five years of their lives together. We did a lot of hiking and exploring in Colorado and saw absolutely beautiful country, but as it sometimes happened, Sis and I would struggle to see eye to eye, and so when I called Dad the last week of July to tell him I thought she was being a bit too bossy, he was quick with a solution.

"No problem, Son, I have a plane ticket for you, and you can start at Stinson's with Stub next Monday."

Yes, I have often wondered what in hell I was thinking when I called Dad to complain.

So anyway, I reported to Stinson Canning Company at 6:00 a.m. the following Monday morning to start my career as a fish processor.

The first task my Unc Stub, now my foreman, assigned to me was the chum truck.

The chum truck was a large wheeler dump truck parked under a scuttle hole in the side of the factory, whose main purpose was to receive all the waste of the herring and mackerel that was being processed.

The waste was dumped into the body of the truck from a conveyor which was 18 inches wide, and stuck up in the air on an angle four feet above the highest point of the body of the truck. This meant the waste made a huge pile in the middle of the body.

Someone had to stand in the body of the truck, and, using a garden rake, spread the waste around the body of the truck so it would fill evenly.

So, adorned in rain-slicker bib overalls, thigh-high rubber boots, rubber gloves, and carrying two garden rakes, (in case the handle broke on one), I clambered up into the body of the truck and joined the very squishy, fishy, mess.

I did mention this was the end of July, right?

The temps were climbing quickly to the 90s that day.

Before 9:00 a.m., I was standing waist deep in this soup trying to keep the level even inside the body of the truck, without staggering under the endless stream of heads, tails, and guts flowing from the conveyor. When that truck was full, I got a ten-minute break while the truck was replaced with another one.

Unc Stub happened by at one point to check on me, peered in the body of the truck, nodded at my work, and asked, "Whatcha think, Mitch?"

I knew this was a trick question. If I told him what I thought, he would likely find something even worse for me to do. So, I grinned and said, "Hey, it's nice to be able to work outside, Unc. Thanks for giving me this job."

Stub chuckled and informed me as he turned to go back inside the factory that "this is building character".

Yeah, right. I was literally up to my ass in "character".

By the way, you might wonder what my compensation for this job was, I was paid $1.40 an hour, no overtime pay, but there was plenty of overtime.

At about 4:30 that afternoon, Unc came out and told me to hop down. The processing lines were almost done for the day, and there was adequate room left in the truck. So, he made me stand over a large grate in the ground that led to the factory's waste disposal system, and he hosed me down with this high pressure 2" water hose that damn near knocked me on my ass. Evidently, I was too smelly even for the fish factory. After that, I was led inside where I helped with the cleaning of the processing lines. Actually that part was fun. I and two other guys my age, were hosing down everything in sight, including each other, and washing it all down into the same waste disposal system. When that was done, Unc told us all, "You boys go home and get some dinner and rest, and then meet me back here at 11:00 p.m."

Herring and mackerel were hauled to the factory in large tanker semi-trucks, or by boat. That night, it was a tanker truck, filled with soon to be sardines. We would use those powerful water hoses to wash the fish from the truck through a sluice into awaiting storage tanks, located in the basement of the factory, for the next day's processing.

I had long since been able to recognize just how awful I smelled. I mean, after a while your body, in its own defense, shuts off your sense of smell.

When I climbed out of Unc's Dodge power-wagon, in my grandparents driveway, intent on going in and enjoying my grandmother's fabulous cooking, and having a much-needed meal, I soon realized the reason why grandmother, Mamie, was widely known for her bloodhound nose.

I didn't even make it to the steps of the shed.

Mamie met me on the steps with a broom and proceeded to whack me with it.

"You are NOT coming into this house smelling like that." Whack, "You get those clothes off out here on the steps." Whack whack, "Then, you get yourself in the shower, and make sure you clean the shower after." Whack.

"Ok, ok Mamie...stop whacking me with that broom."

I looked back towards the driveway to see Unc Stub, sitting in his truck, laughing it up as he backed out of the driveway and headed to his house. I secretly hoped that Aunt Brenda whacked the hell out of him with her broom when he got there.

Then I remembered Unc Stub's words, that this was building character. Boy oh boy, evidently I needed an extra helping of it.

So, I began the now daily ritual of stripping down on the steps of the shed, slinking into the shower inside the shed, usually with a couple of reminder whacks of the broom from my beloved Mamie, and then putting all those offensive smelling clothes in a bag kept in the barn, until Mamie would wash them. She refused to let those clothes come anywhere near any other laundry. Once a week, she would wash my work clothes and then clean and sanitize the washing machine after. I stayed well out of the range of her lethal broom when she did this.

Over the next five weeks, I worked several different jobs at the factory. I would dump the little cans that sardines are packed in onto the belt that would carry them to the ladies that comprised the line. They would grab the cans off from this belt, and fish from another belt that ran round and round, and then they would do their ju-ju magic with scissors and knives, and stuff the finished cleaned fish into these cans, while sweeping all the chum onto yet another belt to be carried out to the chum truck. From there, the cans of packed fish were put on yet another belt which carried them to a huge and very mysterious contraption that washed the fish, then pressure cooked them, and finally sealed the cans, where they would pop out on the other side, ready to be packed for market. This "can-man" job was easy, so I would jump at the chance to do it when the regular can-man wasn't there.

One day, I and another kid my age, Freddie, were carrying large cans of jalapeno peppers, to distribute on the line for a run of jalapeno infused sardines. These cans were gallon sized and the liquid would slop over us as we loaded the line. We wore protective aprons and gloves because the juice would burn and leave an ugly red rash to exposed skin. Freddie told me he had to pee, and asked if I'd cover for him. I told him I would but he should hurry because the two of us were struggling to keep up. He promised to be as quick as he could and ran off to the bathroom. A couple of minutes later a pitiful scream could be heard over the constant loud thrum of the factory at work. Freddie came out of the bathroom, his eyes wide, his face flushed, and he was walking like he was on stilts. Apparently, in his haste to be quick, he didn't bother to wash his hands before unzipping.

Poor Freddie. Not only was he in obvious and constant-twitch pain, but he was teased unmercifully by both the men and the ladies.

Especially the ladies.

"You want me to take a look Freddie? My mother used to be a nurse."

"Hey Freddie, I'm looking for a "hot" date tonight...interested?"

Anyway, I also, at times, would pack the cooked and sealed cans of sardines into boxes in the warehouse located next to the factory. I sometimes would go down into the bowels of the factory to help the bailers. This job was hard physical work. Wielding huge fish nets on long poles, these guys would dip into the large storage tanks of herring floating in water and dump them onto the conveyor belt that would carry the fish upstairs to the processing line. A great workout for the upper body.

There were a couple of guys, Phil and Arthur, that worked the nets that could only be described as colorful. Phil told me he was a descendant of Geronimo himself. And, he would go into sort of a fugue when Arthur would start the "war beat" using the handle of his net on the side of the fish tank. Phil, would get this glazed look in his eyes and start war-dancing, whooping a war cry and scare the living bejesus out of anyone that wasn't aware of their little prank. Newbies to the factory were always indoctrinated by Phil and Arthur, me included.

Hey, I was 15 for crying out loud...I didn't know....until Unc Stub walked in during one of these "fits".

"You boys wanna play around all day, I'll go back upstairs and tell the ladies why there ain't no fish on the line."

The ladies were paid piece-meal. They didn't like empty lines. That was far scarier than a crazy Indian.

Other entertainment on the job down there in the bowels were the rats.

I had never seen rats that big before, some of them as big as a large cat or a small poodle. I guess they thrived on fish chum. Mostly they shied away from humans, but you never wanted to corner one of them. The simple fact was, they were there, and they were not going away. So, I left them alone and they left me alone. Phil and Arthur would store rocks to throw at them, but I figured it would only make 'em meaner, so I didn't participate. Those two were pretty decent shots. I wondered if either one of them ever thought about pitching a baseball.

This five-week odyssey of working at the sardine factory finally came to an end when it was time to go back to school, although I did occasionally continue to go with Unc Stub at night to help unload the fish. Gave me a few bucks for school lunch, and it was worth the dreaded broom of my grandmother. Usually we would return home after unloading fish in the wee hours, and Mamie being annoyed at the hour, would put a little extra into the whack.

After that summer of 1971, I never returned to work at the sardine factory, but I will never forget the experience. After all, it truly did build character.

Story Fifteen

Cat's Cradle

Harry Chapin, the popular singer/songwriter of the 70s once penned a song called "The Cat's in the Cradle". It is a ballad about a man in his retirement years reflecting on his life and his relationship with his son. In the song Harry tells the story of a man who was always caught up in his work and never had time for his son, and later in life, after he was retired, he recognized that because of that, now his son never seemed to have time for him. When I first heard that song, I immediately identified with the message of the song. There seemed to be a lot of similarities between Harry's story of that father/son relationship and my own relationship with my dad.

When I grew up in the 60s, it seemed I had very little time with my dad. Unc Stub was the guy who taught me how to hunt, and the guy who took me hunting and fishing. Unc Stub showed me how to swing the bat, throw a curve ball, and helped me with my first brake job on the old '55 Dodge Coronet field bomb I had. It seemed that Dad never had time, he was always at work. The only exception, it seemed, were the nights Dad and I would spend on the front door steps, radio on, listening to the Red Sox games and tossing the ball back and forth. Other than that Dad was the guy who lectured me, grounded me, criticized me, set the rules and enforced them, and generally made my life miserable.

I suppose someone had to, my mother was rarely able to. She struggled most of her life with afflictions that ranged from alcoholism to drug abuse. She spent almost as much time in one in-house program or another, as she did at home. She was also a regular at the local hospital. She had at least four car wrecks that demolished cars that Dad still owed money on. Auto insurance was minimal in those days and health insurance was either non-existent, or very, very limited. Suffice to say, Dad was hard pressed to keep up with Mom's bills. He never complained about the bills as I recall, he just did what he always did—worked, and then worked some more.

From my earliest recollections my dad has always worked harder than anyone I've ever known. I know, I know—most sons are likely to say that about their fathers. It's all about that father/son hero worship thing that the psychologists like to pontificate on, but I am telling you all that in Dad's case it is a fact.

When I was very young, my earliest memories of Dad always involved him and work. He held at least three jobs all the time. He worked at Northern Chemical, a chemical processing plant, before I was born until I was a teenager. At Northern Chemical Dad was responsible for taking "Bunker C" oil (crude oil) and refining it through a process of scrubbing that I've never been able to fully understand, and by using intense heat of over 3,000 degrees Fahrenheit, liquid ammonia was created. Then the liquid ammonia was further refined to make nitrate acid. I have little knowledge of how all of that was done, but I do know that it was considered highly dangerous work.

At Northern Chemical, one worked shift work—day, night, graveyard shifts, on a rotation, with a number of days off in-between. So it was hard to know when exactly Dad was gonna be around when I was a little kid. Made it really hard to get away with stuff, 'cause you were never sure if Dad might walk around the corner at any given moment.

On top of Northern Chemical, Dad was also the janitor for a local bank, Merrill Trust. He managed to do this job even though his primary job at Northern Chemical was that rotating schedule. That meant that Dad might be cleaning the bank at 5:00 p.m. one day, and then 3:00 a.m. another.

Besides those two jobs, Dad also worked at a local plant and shrub nursery called Cedar Croft Nursery. He discovered he had a green thumb, was a quick learner and was able to recite the names of most any plant, shrub, tree, bush, weed or the green stuff that grows in your refrigerator, in Latin. He still can. I once asked him when I was about 19 if he could tell me the Latin name for marijuana, thinking that it would be really cool and a great way to impress a girl. He replied straight-faced, "Cannabis idiota."

It took a few years before I realized why it never impressed any girls. He was calling me a "pot-head" in Latin.

Another time I recall walking with him and Pup on Mamie's lawn in the late spring where there was a 30'-long hedge of purple lilacs in full bloom, the air redolent with the sweet aroma. Dad, trying to impress ol' "cannabis idiota" and his father, says, "Oh my, Father, aren't your Buddleia davidii beautiful!"

Pup stops, looks at the shrubs, and then at Dad and says, "I'll be damned, all these years I've been calling them things lilacs," shakes his head and walks on.

I snickered.

Dad glared at me and followed Pup into the backyard. I noticed that Dad didn't name the burdocks in Latin that he happened to brush against as he walked past the barn either.

Anyway, besides these three jobs, Dad would help around the farm, haying, shearing sheep, spreading manure, and fencing. Besides that, he always grew a large garden and tended it fiercely, weeds were never ever allowed in Dad's garden. He cut firewood, enough for himself, for me, and for other family members, but also for customers that bought firewood from Dad for many years. Now cutting firewood sounds simple but it is back-breaking, grueling work. I can tell you from experience, that while swamp maple, swamp beech, and swamp birch may be the preferred woods of choice as far as B.T.U.s and heating power is concerned, it is, as its name implies, in a swamp. Hard to cut wood in a swamp, and harder to yard it out in 4' lengths, which was done on a trailer attached to an old John Deere tripod tractor. Sloshing through knee-high water and mud while swatting black flies, arms weary from running the chainsaw and lifting 4' logs as big around as the average truck tire onto the wagon to transport the wood out into the wood yard, to be stacked until there was enough to provide wood to keep our families warm in the upcoming winter, and enough to sell to regular customers, for the money to pay the taxes.

Wait...I ain't done.

Next, the wood had to be cut stove length and split if it was too big to fit inside the stove. Log by log, stick by stick, Dad would plug away, working one pile then the next until it was all done. Then, he would load the wood onto his truck and haul it to the woodsheds of the folks that were to be the recipients of his labors, and then unload it and stack it in their sheds.

Then, and only then, he would fill his own woodshed.

You want more?

Ok, remember Dad's garden?

Dad not only took a lot of pride in growing his garden, he put an immense amount of effort into freezing, canning, and pickling the bounty of that garden, every year, year in and year out. We always had plenty of his veggies in the freezer, as well as shelves of canned and pickled goods in the cellar each winter. There were bags of onions, bins of potatoes and turnip, bags of carrots, and Dad always raised a beef critter and a pig each summer so our freezer was always stocked to the gills with meat as well as a crock of fatback from the pig that he slaughtered, butchered, and wrapped himself. Always. Every year.

Unbelievably, there's more.

He and my youngest uncle, Unc Stub, also built, stocked and maintained a meat shop. In the fall of each year, they would take in deer harvested by hunters and cut and wrap their meat for them. As well, the whole family would have their beef critters, pigs, lamb, and their own deer butchered, cut and wrapped in Dad's and Unc's meat shop.

On top of all that, Dad dug the cellar in our house by hand. In his fleeting spare time, sometimes by lantern after dark, the man would take his pick-axe and shovel and pick away at the rock-hard clay that our house was sitting on because he wanted a full 8' cellar under his house and said he couldn't afford to hire it done.

He dug the well for our house by hand, too. He did all the wiring, plumbing, carpentry, sheet rocking, painting, tiling, oil burner maintenance, as well as all repairs and all renovations to our house, himself. He was his own and the family's mechanic. He shoveled the snow out of our driveway by hand.

My dad has never, ever, not once in his life, missed a day of work due to a hangover, although I know he has gone to work with one more than once. In fact I don't ever recall him missing any day of work for any reason with two exceptions. The first was when he had bronchial pneumonia, and was hospitalized. The second was when he was hospitalized with kidney stones, and then only after he went to work and had to be hauled by ambulance from work to the hospital.

After he left Northern Chemical in the late 60s, Dad went to work for Frost & Wilkins, a heating oil company. Dad began as an oil burner technician and quickly mastered the trade and became the company's service manager. He worked there for 15 years. He kept the janitorial job at the bank during the majority of that time, too. After that he became the building maintenance director for the local tech school, a job he really loved, and did that until he, in his words, "retired", what anyone else would call self-employed. He always had more handyman and carpentry jobs than he could keep up with. Retirement was a very busy time for Dad. Up every morning at 5:00 a.m., breakfast with Pup, off to work, and never home before 5:00 p.m., rain or shine, and usually weekends as well. Dad's biggest problem, as I saw it, was the simple fact that he could do anything, and do it exceptionally well. He was always more than fair with his price, and became fast friends with everyone he did work for. He was in very high demand.

In spite of all this, my Dad found time to indulge himself in hobbies. Those included teaching himself to be a gourmet chef, to build and finish some of the most beautiful furniture I've ever seen, to learn the intricacies of fine wine, and somehow, he always seemed to find time to share our mutual passion for baseball and the Red Sox, with me.

Later in his life, Dad decided to cut back and hold only two jobs, which he did for a long time, and then finally he became something less than Superman and held only one job. But, he still did all of his own house repairs and renovations as well as most of mine and some of my sister, too. He still, to this day, helps my Unc Stub at his saw mill in the summer months and still cuts firewood for me to burn. You see, Dad lives in Florida now, and only comes to Maine for about four months a year. Oh yes, he still works every day while in Florida, he is the de facto maintenance man for the retirement village he lives in.

Growing up, I never went without. I didn't always have the newest bike or the "coolest" snowmobile, but I had a bike and I had a snowmobile. I never went hungry, I always had new clothes every fall to go to school in. I was given money every day for school lunch because I refused to take a bag lunch. When I decided it wasn't cool to ride the school bus anymore, Dad would take me to school on his way to work and drop me off, I was on my own as far as getting home from school, he was still at job one, and had another job to go to after the clock struck 5:00 p.m. while everyone else was going home to their families.

Dad has been married six times, twice to my mother, and other than his house, he got taken to the cleaners every time he divorced. It was, however, nice to have new furniture so often. He finally discovered the love of his life and soul mate, Gloria, about 30 years ago and has been happily married ever since, but he sure did take the path less traveled getting there.

He never, ever, not once in my life, has complained to me about his lot in life.

Later in my life, when I got married and bought an old ramshackle farmhouse in need of almost complete renovations, not only did he do a majority of the work himself, nights and weekends, he used a lot of his own money to complete the work. He has never once mentioned the money he spent on my house, in fact refused to talk about it when I tried to bring it up.

The man is a rock.

Nowadays when I hear that song by Harry Chapin, I still think of Dad, but now I reflect on how I felt when I was a kid, and how things have changed in my perception.

Maybe all those psychologists are right after all.

Or just maybe...he really is a hero.

Story Sixteen

Animal Olympics

One of the more subtle things that I liked to watch as a kid growing up on the three farms my family operated was the "community" that existed between the various breeds of animals, and the even clearer relationship between animals of a common breed. It was interesting to see how the sheep would interact with the cows, or how the horses and ducks got along. To the casual observer, the larger animals went where they wanted and the smaller breeds would move out of their way, otherwise they would tend to ignore each other.

Not always the case.

The pecking order on the farm was not necessarily breed specific, although sometimes it was.

For example, horses were the kings of the pasture. They were the largest, strongest, fastest, and one of the more intelligent of the animals. The cows intermingled easily enough with the horses as they offered no aggression towards the horses, or anything or anyone else either. In fact, the horses would typically look after the cows and would alert them to the fact something was askew, such as someone walking through the pasture on his way to the creek with a fishing pole over his shoulder. The horses would watch intently, while the cows seemed not to notice. They would be contentedly chewing away at the green grass. However, if the horses felt encroached upon or nervous and started moving away from the stranger in the pasture, the cows would dutifully follow them to another section.

If a bull in season was added to the mix, the horses basically figured the cows were on their own and stayed far away. It's kinda funny, 11 months of the year, most of the bulls we had were as docile and, frankly, as stupid as the cows, but when they were in season, they became highly combative and were to be avoided. I remember one day when I was a teenager I was at Unc Gene's farm, and I decided to climb a golden delicious apple tree inside the pasture about 30 feet from the road. My intent was to snag a few of those delicious apples. As it happened, this bull we called ol' Blue took offense to the fact I was in his crib. He decided to express his displeasure by head-butting the tree I was in, and then he decided to wait me out, pawing and snorting at the base of the tree.

Cousin Genie and Unc Gene thought this was highly entertaining as they were watching from the porch and laughing it up.

I figured I wouldn't starve at least, the apples were really, really good. Ironically, I was in this predicament because I figured it would score me some brownie points with Unc Gene, as these were his favorite apples, and I had intended to take him a few of the more pristine ones.

The two of them did attempt to be helpful however as Genie hollered over, "Jump down on his back and ride him."

I recall that I dropped a fantastically perfect apple accidentally when I gave Cuz the ol' one finger salute at this suggestion.

The apple, in fact, bounced off the head of Ole Blue, which was akin to throwing a cotton ball at a rock. It did, however, give me an idea. I figured maybe I could entice the bull to chase after a few apples and forget about me. I didn't need much, it was only 30 feet to the gate.

Life lesson number 9989—bulls don't eat apples or chase them.

Life lesson number 9990—one should never start throwing a bunch of Unc's favorite apples all over the pasture.

At least Unc stopped laughing at me and made Genie send his dog, Rex, into the pasture to yap and drive Ole Blue back to the herd of cows some 300 feet away in the lower end of the pasture.

None of the animals messed with the dog. The dog was the uber drill sergeant of the farmyard. And, I didn't mess with Unc Gene. I had to retrieve all the apples I threw...all the while keeping a wary eye on Blue.

It's important to note here that my family also operated a farm we dubbed the "Other Farm" which abutted Unc Gene's farm. The Other Farm was where most of the livestock were kept, and the animals could easily be moved from one pasture or one farm to another. These two farms totaled about 350 acres of pasture, hayfields, a couple of farm ponds, a fantastic trout stream, and about 100 acres of forest, or as we say here in Maine, "woods". It remains, to this day, the most beautiful land in this county.

Anyway, watching the sheep was another interesting slice of barnyard culture. The sheep typically stayed together in a scattered cluster but off to themselves. Sheep are one of the most defenseless animals I've ever known, and so they tend to stay away from all other animals, which is somewhat of a paradox. They would be much safer if they stayed amongst the other animals. This became an ever increasing problem as the coyote population here in Maine continued to grow through the 1970s.

Coyotes terrorized the sheep, on occasion, killing several in a night. To further complicate the problem, coyotes are incredibly resourceful, very intelligent, and almost impossible to stop. They are too smart to be trapped, poisoning them was out of the question, and hunting them was almost laughable. The only real option was to let them come to you, which meant spending many nights sitting in the old '49 Willy's jeep, hidden in the bushes, on the edge of the pasture, with high-powered rifles, hoping for enough moonlight to pick one up in the scope. Coyotes hunt at night, another sign of their cleverness. They usually hunted in packs of three or four, but sometimes there would be only one. They are very fast, ruthless and fearless.

Typically, they would make the kill quickly, eat the organs (the heart, lungs and liver), and then escape to the woods to hunt another night. They would come in cycles, never staying in the same patch of woods or feasting off the same farm for more than a few nights—very clever animals. Unc Gene discovered a way to tell if his sheep were going to be attacked that night, which I have always thought epitomizes the term "good ol' Yankee ingenuity". He came to realize that vultures would begin to flock to the farm and perch on the fences at the edge of the woods just before dark. Unc understood that the vultures followed the coyotes and would feast on the remains of the kill once the coyotes had their fill and had run off into the woods. Unc Gene and Cousin Genie were both excellent marksmen and shot many coyotes over the course of time. Some of us other men in the family would take our turns from time to time and join them in the all-night vigil of protecting the herd. We were basically there to just offer company. The real responsibility of sitting there, night after long night, always fell on their shoulders. Still, they would be on the farm the next day, working side by side with the others.

The only time the sheep would naturally intermingle with the other animals was during winter months when they couldn't graze. Then they were forced to eat from the common piles of hay we tossed out from the barn each morning and night. The sheep had a very noticeable community within the flock. I always marveled at how a mother sheep and her lambs could distinguish each other's bleats from the cacophony of hundreds of such bleats in this cluster of over 400 head. I also found it very heartwarming when a mother sheep would accept a lamb, whose mother had not survived, as her own. That didn't always happen. In fact, it was not common, but it happened enough to appreciate the community of these sheep. More often, one of us kids would become the surrogate mother to a little lamb who had lost its mother, bottle feeding it until it was grown enough to fend for itself.

It was the lambs that were such a joy to watch. Sheep typically have twins, sometimes a single lamb, and occasionally triplets, but most often, it is twins. When the lambs are very young they stay very close to Mom, and the brother/sister tandems become inseparable. They tend to chase each other around, work their head-butting skills on each other, vie for Mom's attention and her milk, and generally seem to be getting a big kick out of life. They even appear to be smiling joyfully as they bleat and jump, kicking up their heels and wiggling their tails.

In the eastern-most pasture beside the road at the Other Farm was an old manure pile. This pile had been there for years, and over the course of time it had thousands of hooves to compact it to a 4-foot knoll in the middle of that pasture. It was about 30 feet in diameter, and the surrounding ground was very flat, so it was a landmark of sorts.

Just before dark, in the late spring of the year, all the lambs would gather in a big circle around this pile. The lambs were about two months old by this time and had become very agile and incredibly playful. These lambs would circle this knoll and then it would start.

Games of tag.

Two or three of the lambs would rush at each other over the top of the pile and then run back to their place in the circle. Then another two or three would do the same, and so on. This game they played was incredibly orderly. They seemed to be showing off for each other, to see who could jump the highest and click his hooves together or who could wiggle his tail the most vigorously. Sometimes they would jump over each other and chase each other in circles around one of the pear trees, all the while bleating happily. The mother ewe would stand back 20' or so from the circle to oversee the affair and watch their young 'uns play. Then as darkness fell over the barnyard, the mama ewe and her lambs would find each other and look for a hollow or an alcove of bushes, or that prime property in behind the old hay conveyor for the night's lodging accommodations. They would lie snuggled up with each other in a circle, and the farmyard would become almost silent as the little ones first nursed and then drifted off to sleep, dreaming the dream of baby lambs.

Watching this animal Olympics never failed to validate, for me, all that is pure and naturally beautiful in life. It made me feel good to be alive and always made me realize how fortunate I was to be part of this farm and this family. It still remains one of the sweetest memories of my youth.

It actually became quite a pastime for a lot of folks around here. On many early evenings the driveway leading into the Other Farm would have several vehicles sitting there with a family inside, eating ice cream cones and watching the lambs play their bedtime games.

I believe that if all of us had the opportunity to take a half hour at the end of the day and spend it with our family, friends, and neighbors watching those lambs rejoice in the simple beauty of life, we would appreciate our own lives more.

Story Seventeen

Watch Out

It has been a long standing tradition for the Maine native to hunt. Most generational families here in Maine have lots of stories of Grandpa or the Uncs that involve shooting deer, moose, bear, rabbits, squirrels, partridge, pheasant, ducks, turkey, woodcock, and other assorted game. This activity is/was not only a great source of entertainment, fellowship, and opportunity to pass down the acquired skills and woodsmanship from generation to generation, but a great resource of very tasty and natural meat products for the family dinner table.

Now I must warn you PETA types, you 'back to earth' tree-huggers, and you vegans, this story may not be for you. You could go save a whale and buy the current edition of Mother Earth instead, but, if you really want to go green, listen up, I'll tell you the way it really was, and you might learn something in the process.

First, hunting is not bad. Hunting is good. Hunting has always been a basic and natural course of events in the entire history of mankind. You would not be here if man did not hunt. It is instinctive and it is necessary. If, for whatever reason, you cannot wrap your mind around this very simple but entirely accurate concept, then please do not read any further. Go eat some prunes and cleanse your colon or whatever it is you folks do to purge such ideas from your finicky little minds.

Easy there big Mitch!

I'm joking, sorta, I needed to find a way to work in the phrase "cleanse your colon". You'll see, it's worth it.

Second, nature's bounty—namely the a aforementioned bear, deer, moose, rabbits, partridge, pheasant, squirrels, ducks, woodcock, turkey, and other assorted game, is the most natural, healthiest, and in my opinion, the tastiest meat anyone could ever eat. Most folks I know whose meat intake is a high percentage of wild game never need a colon cleansing as that happens naturally. As it should. These folks also tend to have a very strong affinity with ol' Ma Nature, and want to preserve her land, her bounty, and the timeless tradition that has been passed down for thousands of years. Some things just can't be improved upon. Further, some things cannot be learned in the hallowed halls of Yale, but must be learned by participating, being taught by your elders and experiencing the natural ebb and flow of the food chain first-hand. These people are the true experts, and can better educate us all on what is proper and what is not.

There! That's my rant, now on to the story.

Growing up on the family farm, wild game was an almost daily supplement to our diet. We depended on it. We were a farm family and could not afford to buy our meat in the grocery store. True, we did raise beef cattle, sheep, chickens, pigs, and domestic turkeys, and oh yes, we did feed ourselves from our livestock, but, the livestock was also one of our sources of income. So, wild game was what we ate, at least as much, as the meat we raised. I still prefer a nice piece of back strap off a deer that I or one of my family members has harvested, over the local grocery store's highly expensive cut of rib eye that had growth hormones injected into the critter it came from, any day.

Twice on Sunday.

Anyway, we ate a lot of venison when I grew up. This meant that the venison we ate was not always legal. Back then, it was an unspoken rule or agreement that a family that needed the meat for the dinner table would usually cause the authorities and game wardens to sorta look the other way. Now you should be aware that I am talking about people who harvested the deer to eat, the entire deer. Not just shoot them for sport. Most of the people I am describing were also pretty clever about harvesting meat for their families without anyone else knowing about it. Along those lines, it was pretty common for the women of the family to "tag out" in the first week of the deer season, so the men could continue to hunt legally. Once again, a practice that was most often met with the local game warden sorta turning his head the other way, as it was understood the meat was needed and was not being wasted.

Most of the time…but not always.

For years the local game warden was a man called Gil, being how his last name was Gilpatrick, but everyone just called him Gil. He was a good man, a fine father, a great neighbor, and well respected member of our community. He was also a very good game warden. He knew when to apply his professional duty and when to avert his eyes. He would often take deer, or other game, he had seized from poachers, to families that needed the meat. He helped his community the best way he could. Then one day, he retired. A new game warden was assigned to cover the territory that Gil had presided over for so many years. This new fella was young, ambitious, and didn't come from around here.

Bad recipe, for sure.

He, this new fella, was determined to make a name for himself and force his way to game warden super-stardom. He made enemies real fast, alienated just about everyone in the area, and was fond of intimidating and harassing people who he thought had broken one of the various laws regulating hunting and fishing. He was sneaky and clever, and would try and set people up so he could then arrest them.

Clearly, he needed his colon cleansed.

For the purpose of this story, I am going to refer to our inflamed colon game warden as Dewey, not his real name, but a name that seemed to fit this guy. My sincerest and most humble apology to all the Deweys in the world.

Anyway, my cousin Ron was really looking forward to deer season this particular year. He had planned ahead, got all his work caught up so he could take the time to hunt for the entire month of November. He had done his homework, scouted the area, found the "beds" the deer seem to be using, watched their movement, their patterns, when they were feeding, and on what. He had cleaned his rifle, lined up the scope to be sure it was precise; he had washed his hunting clothes in a special detergent to nullify the human scent. He had practiced "rattling" with an old set of antlers from a deer that was harvested a few years back. He was ready. He was a happy man.

He was up before dawn that first morning of deer season, ate a breakfast of leftover baked beans and some deer steak from last year's bounty, along with some extra strong coffee. He dressed in his hunting garb, gave the rifle a final wipe-down, checked his clips and made sure he had extra ammunition, turned off the kitchen light and stepped out the door onto the porch. He stood for a moment to let his eyes adjust and watched as his breath created plumes of vapor in the cold morning air. He scanned the edge of the back pasture and his heartbeat jumped! There, on the back edge of the pasture were two young doe grazing. He evened his breathing, looked them over with his scope and considered the situation. The family needed the meat, and he knew that no matter how well he had planned, there was an even chance he would not get a chance like this again this season. So he fired two quick shots that both found their mark. He walked out to the two deer and saw that both had died instantaneously. He field dressed them and dragged them, one at a time, back to the barn, a hundred yards away. While he did this he had an idea. Perhaps his mother, my Aunt Edie, could tag one of the deer, and maybe his grandfather Ivory would consider tagging the other. That way he could still hunt, hell, it wasn't even an hour into the season. So he went back into the house and woke his mother. Aunt Edie said she would be happy to tag the deer, but she would need to go to town first.

"Go to town?" Cousin Ron inquired, "Why?"

"Well," said Aunt Edie, "I probably should have a hunting license before I try to tag that deer, don't-cha think?" Ron agreed and said he would walk down to his grandfathers to see if he was willing to tag the other doe. Then they waited until 8:00 a.m. for the town office to open so the hunting license could be purchased.

When the clock struck 8:00 a.m., Ron, Aunt Edie, and Ivory pulled into the parking lot of the old school that served as the town office and Aunt Edie went in and purchased a combination hunting/fishing license.

"12 dollars," she groused, as she climbed back into the pickup, "highway robbery is what that is."

Cousin Ron drove back to the farm and loaded the two deer onto the back of the pickup and proceeded to the tagging station, located at the little country general store our family frequented as it was out of the city and was supported mostly by the local farm families. Bowen's Store was a small ram-shackled building that was packed with just about everything a family needed, from groceries, gas, beer, tobacco, baling twine, penny candy, soda pop, hunting supplies, ice cream, "Eye-talian" sandwiches, the local newspaper, to gum rubber boots and work gloves. Harry Bowen, the proprietor, was a curmudgeonly older gent who typically wore a t-shirt that stated "Yes, I am a native, and NO I don't give directions." His store was located out in the country, but was on one of the major roads leading into town, so he did see his share of "flat-landers" pulling in, not to buy anything from his store, but to ask "Say...can you tell me how to get to..." You see his store from the outside looked more like an old falling down motor vehicle repair shop, with the old-fashioned gas pumps off to the side, and an even older, more falling down barn behind the gas pumps. The building featured siding that looked more like asphalt shingles that belonged on the roof, in sort of a brown/reddish plaid pattern, complete with assorted holes and tears here and there to complete that 1940s vintage shack look. Harry didn't believe in the concept of advertising, because there was very little, if any, signage on the outside of the building, just a faded ancient neon sign propped on the peak of the roof that proclaimed "Bowen's".

The inside was dark and a bit dingy, as every source of outside light, the windows, were plugged with hanging cardboard displays of assorted sundry items. The floors were grimy hardwood that sloped every which way, and the countertop which held the cash register in front of the cigarette and chewing tobacco display was old chipped Formica that was stained so bad I don't know its original color or pattern. I do know that it held the best damn sour pickles and pickled pigs feet in gallon jars that I may have ever eaten, store bought, that is.

Anyway, Harry decided that if these tourists that kept asking directions couldn't purchase anything from his store, that he would forget how to get anywhere. Hell, they could at least buy some gas and one of them new-fangled "Eye-talian" sandwiches he had started to make in his store. I'm not sure Harry ever knew what a pizza was, much less gourmet coffee.

No-sah!

In any case, Bowen's was our all-purpose store, and luckily we never needed to depend on Harry for directions.

By this time, it was going on 8:30, as Ron pulled into Bowen's with his mother and grandfather. Harry came out and looked over the two deer splayed out in the back of the pickup, commented, "Ain't all that big, but you just know them's gonna be damn tasty."

He filled out the two tags, had Aunt Edie and Ivory sign in the appropriate spots, and tied a tag on each deer's ear. Ron paid the tagging fee of $2 per deer, to which Aunt Edie once again proclaimed, "Damned highway robbery," to which Harry responded, "Edie, you know I only get $1 of that, the State gets the other $1."

"Well, Harry, you and the State do have a lot in common." Aunt Edie drawled as she got into the pickup and shut the door.

With that, Cousin Ron pulled out onto the road, leaving Harry standing in his parking lot blinking and thinking that one over. They went back to the farm and hung the two deer up in the barn, side by side, with the heads down so the precious hind-quarters would not retain any blood. The deer would be allowed to hang for two days to cure then the hide would be stripped and the animals would be butchered, packaged, and put into the freezer for the upcoming long and cold winter.

Mmmmm...a supper of back-strap, sauteed in a seasoned cast iron frying pan with onions and mushrooms, along with a steamed winter squash from the garden, a spoonful or two of homemade corn relish, and of course, hot biscuits fresh out of the kitchen woodstove oven with homemade butter and a dab of home preserved raspberry jam on them, makes for a mighty fine dinner while basking in the warmth of the crackling fire of the woodstove as the winter wind moans outside and snow pelts the windows.

Sounds pretty cozy, don't it?

It is.

Oh...I forgot one thing...one should always take the pan drippings from the frying pan and drizzle them on the squash. Now you got yourself a meal fit for kings and queens.

So, back to our story, not long after Cousin Ron had the two deer hung up in the barn, while he and Aunt Edie were stacking some firewood for the kitchen stove on the back porch, a green pickup truck came bouncing into the yard kicking up a cloud of dust. The truck had the insignia of the Maine State Game Warden Service on the side of the door, and inside was our friend Dewey. Dewey jumped out and struts up to the porch, his eyes shifting back and forth as if he'd lost something and was looking for it. He had a notepad in his hand and referred to it before he asked, "Is this where an Edie Young lives?"

Aunt Edie glanced at him, uttered a "Heyuh", turned her back to him and continued to stack wood.

Dewey clears his throat and asks, "Are you Edie Young?"

Aunt Edie finished stacking the wood she had in her arms before replying, "Yep, that's me, what can I do for ya?"

"I was doing some checking into things and saw that you tagged a deer this morning at Bowen's Store."

"I did."

"Well, I'd like to see it."

"Sure!...be happy to show you the deer...right down in the barn, follow me."

Aunt Edie and Cousin Ron lead Dewey to the barn, where her husband, Ron's dad, Wilford, was just finishing up the barn chores.

"Willie, this fella here is the new local game warden, and he wants me to show him that deer I shot this morning."

Willie nods at the game warden, then drawls, "Well, Mother, unless it has come back to life, ought to be hanging right where you left it on the other end of the barn."

They all proceeded to the other end of the barn and sure enough the two deer were hanging right where they had left them. Dewey asked, "Which one is yours?"

Aunt Edie pointed to one of them. Dewey inspected the deer and read the tag hanging off the left ear, "Says this one was tagged by Ivory Young," to which Aunt Edie responds, "Well then, it's the other one."

Dewey's eyes widened, "You don't even know which deer you tagged?"

"Both doe, both the same size, if it ain't that one, then it's the other...a deer is a deer."

Dewey figures he's onto something now and asks, "Can you show me the rifle you used and load and unload it for me?"

Cousin Ron passed Aunt Edie his .270. She proceeded to load and unload it flawlessly. Somewhat agitated, Dewey spits out, "How do I know you can even shoot a gun?"

Aunt Edie cocks a grin and replies, "Why don't you walk down in the pasture about a hunnert yards, hold up your watch, and we'll find out."

Dewey's face gets a little red and he blinks and thinks a minute. "How is it that you bought a combination hunting/fishing license at 8:06 a.m. this morning, and shot and tagged a deer by 8:30 a.m.!?"

Aunt Edie never blinked, "Don't take long to pull a trigger."

Dewey had had enough. As he stomped back to his truck, he declared, "You haven't heard the last of this!"

Aunt Edie yawned and scratched her back by rubbing up against the edge of the barn door frame, "Well, I've been living in this very spot for over 40 years, you found me once, I guess you can again."

Dewey spun his tires and he raced out of the yard, creating another big cloud of dust, while Cousin Ron, Aunt Edie, and Willie all watched and chuckled. Dewey never came back around again, in fact it wasn't long after that he requested a transfer to another territory and moved away.

My guess is Aunt Edie probably had herself a good little chuckle every time she cooked a piece of meat off that deer.

Story Eighteen

In Hot Water

*in hot water (with someone) (about someone or something)
Fig. in trouble. (*Typically: be ~; get [into] ~.) You are
going to get into hot water with Rebecca about that. Amy got
into hot water about Todd with Rebecca. John got himself into
hot water by being late.*

Growing up on the farm here in "Podunk" Maine was always
exciting, at least to me. I mean there were so many things to do,
so much to see, plenty of "hot water" to be found.

And, I did...perhaps a little too often.

There seemed to be plenty of opportunity for me to exercise
my fertile imagination throughout the acres of farmland, woods,
streams, orchards, tote roads, gravel pits, farm ponds, abandoned
shacks and camps, barns, chicken houses, junked farm vehicles,
and of course that favorite maple tree that hung out over the road
I lived on. One could climb the tree, skinny out on a huge branch
overhanging the road and watch vehicles pass underneath you.
Pretty exciting stuff!

My elders encouraged me, daily in fact, to contain my
imagination to this vast playground where I seemingly could not
get into, or cause too much trouble.

Ha!...I always found a way.

It's a gift.

Yes, thanks to that fertile imagination, and my natural ability
to create havoc in the most placid of situations, I acquired the
nick-name of "Dennis th' Menace" early in life.

Oh, I was lovable, people in the neighborhood would always
smile when they saw me coming, but it was often accompanied
by a slight cringe.

I'd hear nervous little whispered asides like, "Dear, Mitch is here, why don't you put everything breakable on the top shelf...quickly!" or, "Do you know where the cat is?"

You get the picture.

Anyway, by the time I reached teen-hood, I had pretty much exhausted the entire neighborhood, and had built quite a resume. It was discussed and decided that I needed to experience some culture, see a bit of the world outside of our little hamlet, to see if the rest of the world could survive this little devil.

So, when I was 14, I was "allowed" to go and spend the summer vacation with Sis.

My sister, who is seven years older than me, flew the coup as soon as she graduated from high school, got herself educated, saw some of the country, and ended up getting married while attending college in Kansas.

I think my elders felt like she'd had a long enough break, it was her turn.

So, I went to stay with her and her husband Steve, that summer, in Philadelphia.

Philadelphia....the city of brotherly love, right?

Heh...not for long.

Let's see...it's been 40 years...so, I might be allowed back now. Not sure.

Philadelphia...what an incredibly eye-opening adventure for a 14-year-old hayseed from Maine!

I saw amazing things for the first time ever. The city was beautiful, exciting, loud, flashy, throbbing with life, and endless.

Some of my first: Hare Krishnas, cheese steaks, hot dog vendors, Independence Hall, art museums, sky scrapers, oodles of people of so many ethnic backgrounds...some who spoke in different languages, places open 24 hours a day...I mean! "Toto, we are definitely not in Belfast anymore."

It was incredible...overwhelming. I loved it!

Sis and Steve lived in the northeast sector of the city where there were miles upon miles of row houses—essentially large brick apartment buildings. Street upon street of buildings that were exactly alike. I thought this could present a problem. How would you know if you were even on the right street, let alone the right building, and then how to find the right apartment in this building which contained 10-15 or more apartments?

Mind boggling.

Took me a few days, but I got the gist of it, managed to find my way to the local convenience store, or the neighborhood park and back without busting into the wrong apartment.

Sis and Steve both worked for a large food packing company. They would leave in the morning early, and return around 5:00 p.m. or so. Of course Sis would give me a list of do's and do not's each and every morning before she would, somewhat trepidatiously, leave me in their apartment for the day...alone...unsupervised. Heck, she made me recite the list...three times! Each morning...

By the way...the do not's outnumbered the do's, 10-1.

Their apartment was on the second floor, and the apartment directly underneath us on the ground floor was the home of an older Jewish couple. Such nice folks. I don't remember what the man's name was, but I surely remember the lady's. Her name was Myrna, and she was pretty exotic to me, she would tell me stories about her life that amazed me and set my imagination in high gear. She became the defacto adult supervision for me while Sis and Steve were at work.

She never stood a chance. Sis should have known better...I blame her.

So anyway, I decided one day, in the spirit of being a good and helpful little brother, to clean the apartment, stem to stern. I just knew Sis would be so happy, and that meant maybe I wouldn't have to recite that stupid list every morning.

So, I analyzed the situation...hmmm...let's see, two bedrooms, a living room, the bathroom, and the eat-in kitchen...no sweat...I can knock this out in no time.

I figured that the first thing to do was to fill the sink with hot water and dish detergent. Let the dishes soak while the hot water cooled enough to let me put my hands in it without getting scalded, while I started cleaning some of the other rooms.

Who knew that Philadelphia has such scalding hot water?...I mean scalding...yikes!

Oh yeah...you readers can utter the obligatory "uh oh" now...

You knew it was coming...

For some reason, at that precise moment in time, the faucet, that turned the hot water on and off for the kitchen sink, decided to retire...yep...up and moved to Florida...

Well, ok...it didn't move to Florida...but it didn't work either. I mean it worked just fine when I turned the water on...but then it would NOT TURN OFF!!!!

The knob just spun round and round...the water...the very, very hot water...kept flowing.

The water was so hot I couldn't stick my hand in to pull the plug...

The sink was filling, rather rapidly...what to do?...use that good ol' farm-boy logic Littlefield...THINK!

Just as the sink began to overflow...I had an idea...I gotta shut off the water in the basement!

I ran pell-mell down the stairs to the basement...found the water main...and shut that puppy down!

Ha!...crisis averted...with a little self pat on the back, and a confident little smirk on my face, I climbed the stairs back to the apartment.

"Crisis averted"...heh...not quite.

I did mention that the sink was starting to overflow as I went to the basement, right?

I also mentioned that Myrna, the nice lady who lived downstairs, lived directly under our apartment, didn't I?

As I was mopping up all that water on the kitchen floor...I began to hear voices...lots of voices. None of them sounded happy...there was no "brotherly love" in those voices.

I was able to connect the dots rather quickly. There's a reason why it's called a water main.

And, a tiled kitchen floor is not watertight.

So, between the people hollering because the water stopped running while they were shampooing their hair in the shower, to the guy who just wanted to water his plants, I heard this mournful cry...

"My clothes...all my beautiful clothes...oh no...they are all RUINED!"

This was before Southwest Air was in existence...too bad...I coulda used them. I surely wanted to "get away".

Evidently, the scalding hot water that overflowed the sink, leached through the floor tile and found its way to the ceiling of sweet old Myrna's clothes closet. Yes, it was not pretty, collapsed sheet rock ceiling along with the accompanying dust and dirt of who knows how many eons, all over her precious wardrobe.

Oh boy...Sis was NOT gonna be happy. Well, NO ONE was happy...but Sis and Steve were about to come home to a row house that was akin to a session of Congress (well, after all this WAS Philadelphia)...everyone hollering and gesturing...no one listening...ugh.

I checked the list, overflowing the sink and collapsing the closet ceiling to the apartment under ours, and shutting off the water to the entire building, wasn't on the do not's side, sadly, it was not on the do's side either. Even I was having a difficult time conjuring up a passable excuse.

The ensuing evening was interesting to say the least. Somehow Sis and Steve were allowed to stay and live in their apartment, but the little $%#*&^#...err, I mean...brother...had to go. I think the hat was passed among the building residents to drum up the airfare. Lots of tongue lashings, and finger shaking were dispensed, and I realized that the farm back in Maine had to be missing me, and it was time I went back to where I was needed most, which is the same as, back to where they at least wouldn't kill or maim me, right?

Actually, I did go back to Philadelphia once, while Sis and Steve were still living there, in the same apartment even.

Mom and I drove down for Christmas one year. I dressed as Santa so no one in the building would recognize me.

I'm pretty clever that way, you know.

Story Nineteen

Shear Delight

Growing up on the family farms in the 1960s offered many "Waltonesque" moments. We were a large family that loved each other, worked hard to maintain the farms, and spent most of our time together. So, there were countless moments in time, within the daily events of working these farms that left undeniable impressions on me, and memories that I now love to take out, blow the dust off, and try to recapture. While there were certainly many parts of that life that can be compared to the romantic/idyllic nature of a TV family like the Waltons, it's only fair to understand we were very real, and much more...uh...let's say..."earthy". Now, while in the kitchen of my grandmother, Mamie, one minded his P's and Q's, watched his language, washed his hands, and used proper table manners. On the other hand, while out in the fields, the barns, chicken houses, or in the woods, working beside my grandfather and the uncs...well, let's just say, I learned a whole new vocabulary and perception of life in general. The day was typically filled with little songs and ditties, usually x-rated, sung or recited by my grandfather, and an endless stream of bawdy jokes and limericks vocalized by the uncs. This made the work at hand a little more interesting as it kept the mood light, kept us all chuckling or downright laughing...and usually the dirty little dittie was something of a parable, a lesson, if you will.

Education, farm style.

Also, it's important to note that sympathy, as my Unc Stub was fond of saying, "is found right between shit and syphilis in the dictionary." No whining was allowed, no feeling sorry for oneself was expected. In fact if you did mope or whine, you had better be prepared to be mocked, made fun of, and sometimes even ridiculed, and it was expected that you return the favor at every opportunity. Sort of a family male bonding type of thing. Don't get me wrong, we were a tight-knit family and stood as one. This was all good-natured and light-hearted, and if an outsider made such comments about any one of us, he would feel the stony stares from each of us. Point is, we kept life interesting, and we kept our minds working as hard as our bodies.

Of the endless tasks and chores that are inherent to farm life, perhaps the most grueling was the shearing of the sheep. The sheep population ranged from as low as 200 to as high as 600, depending. Sheep were a viable source of income for the farm. Each spring as many as 300 or more lambs would be born, and most all the males and at least half of the females would be sold to market. Occasionally we would keep a young buck who was thought to be "stud" material, and we would keep enough of the little ewes to replenish the herd.

The other source of income from the sheep was their wool. The task of shearing the wool from the sheep was done in June of each year, and it would typically take two to three weeks to go through the entire herd, along with shearing a few of the neighbors' 4-H projects. It was quite a process. We would first round up all the livestock into the large holding pen adjacent to the barn, separate out and release all the animals except the sheep, and then through a series of gates and movable fences we would drive 15-20 sheep into a smaller holding pen inside the barn. On the outside of this holding pen was a large, long bench set up to hold all the equipment and supplies needed to complete the task at hand. This included sets of electric shears, buckets of hot water to clean the shears/blades, a bucket of tar and brush, grease pencils, a neutering device, a stainless steel tube with a plunger used to worm the animals, a few sharp knives, a device to trim the hooves, and assorted ointments, worm medicine, and powders. My grandfather would man this bench and make sure the shears were always sharp and clean. He would act as the "head nurse" and was in charge of passing whichever tool, device, or product was necessary, over the fence to either me or my cousin. My cousin, Genie-bub, and I acted as assistants to my two uncles, who did the actual shearing and neutering. I would usually be Unc Stub's assistant while Genie did the same for his father, my Unc Gene. We would always lay two 4x8 sheets of plywood on the floor of this holding pen, and abut them to each other. These were for the two shearers to stand on while they did their work. Genie and I would then go grab a sheep or lamb, drag it over to the plywood and pick it up and sit it on its rump with its back leaning against the legs/knees of the shearer. Sheep are very docile animals, and usually once they are sitting on their rumps leaned against the shearers legs, they just submit to whatever is being done to them…"usually".

Folks, these were farm animals, not pets, keep that in mind.

They were not "domesticated". Like most animals, they would take any opportunity to get free if they felt they could. So, even though sheep tend to be quite submissive and docile, they were not happy with the situation.

Part of our job as assistants, was to hold the legs of the sheep if they kicked or thrashed, while the shearer trimmed their hooves, sheared the wool, stuck the long stainless steel wormer down the sheep's throat and gave them a shot of juice, or when the sheep was rolled to the side to complete the shearing around its rump. Sometimes, the sheep would need a little convincing to remain submissive and docile. Anyway, after that was all done, we would apply ointment and then tar to cuts or abrasions. You might be surprised how quickly a sheep heals when it has been nicked while being sheared, Pup always said it was because of the lanolin.

The lambs were a different matter entirely. They did not get sheared, but the males did get neutered, and the lambs going to market would have their tails cropped. This process, while done humanely, was still a bit heart-wrenching because the lambs would bleat pitifully as they were being forced to submit to this process. Can't say I blame them, we would all usually wince a bit ourselves.

So, you get the picture, this was very grueling, hot, sweat running in your eyes, back-breaking work, punctuated by thousands of swarming flies constantly pestering us as we toiled through the day. Once a sheep was sheared, hooves trimmed, wormed, anointed, and released, the wool was wrapped and bundled and added to these huge denim sacks, which eventually we would load onto the truck and haul to the woolen mills to sell.

Then the process would start over again. Another sheep, then another, etc. We were fortunate to have a clear, cold, natural spring near the barn which provided the sweetest water I've ever drank, and we drank lots of it to replenish what our bodies were pumping out in sweat. At lunch time we would take a break and sit under three huge maple trees that lined the drive into the farm. There was a grassy knoll that was shaded by these maples, and a perfect spot to eat cucumber sandwiches, sharp cheese, and drink a cold beer or two for our lunch. During these lunch breaks there would be stories of bygone days of shearing sheep, ribald tales of past adventures that took place on the farm when the uncs were in their mid-teens like Genie-bub and I currently were. Of course, all of this was designed to elicit some embarrassment from the two teenaged boys, to which we would usually just grin and bear it. One particular lunch break I recall, a neighbor, about the same age as my grandfather, by the name of Speck, was helping out for the day, and he commented while slowly chewing on his cucumber sandwich.

"Henry, I noticed three sheep in the pen with ribbons around their necks...one red, one blue, the other yellow...I figured you must have marked them for a reason?"

These sheep, in fact, were there to be sheared, but were owned by neighbors, and the ribbons represented their placing in the local 4-H contest. Of course Speck knew this, so Genie and I knew we were being set up for something.

Henry, with a twinkle in his eye, replied "Well, yes Speck, those three represent the three best sheep in the herd if a fella was to get lonely." Then he winked at Genie and I.

Taking the bait Speck ponders, "Well, gee Henry, with these two 15-year-old young studs here, I would think you would want to keep that sort of critical information to yourself," followed by a hearty smirk thrown in Genie's and my direction.

Henry rubbed his chin and nodded, "Well, yeah, I thought of that, but on the other hand I didn't want to have to go through the entire herd again to find the best three."

I was thinking, "This is as bad as the boys' gym locker at school," where, in fact, Genie and I were teased unmercifully about being "sheep lovers". Ahh well, all in the life of a farm boy.

So anyway, Unc Stub came to the rescue and slapped me on the back and said, "C'mon boys, we better get back to work before you two start getting ideas."

We returned to the barn and started the process over again.

By 3:00 we were all tired, hot, and sweaty. Tempers and dispositions were getting strained along with our backs. Then something happened that I had never seen before. Unc Stub was bent over this sheep, shearing her underside and she was thrashing a little, uncomfortable with the procedure, and frightened. He was spouting out an incredible mix of profanity while trying to hold the thrashing sheep as he sheared. I tried to help by holding her back legs as she sat on her rump with her head stuffed in Unc's crotch.

The sheep BIT him!

I'd never seen a sheep bite before...but she did...she bit him on the tender inside of his upper thigh. Uh WOW!...the shears, the sheep, and the...ahem...shit...flew through the air while Unc redoubled his efforts to spout every profanity known to man.

He may have even invented a few new ones.

After a couple of minutes both the sheep and Unc Stub calmed down. We were all chuckling...teased Unc a little of course...couldn't pass up an opportunity like this. So, I brought the almost-sheared sheep back over to the plywood, reset her on her rump and leaned her against Stub's legs. He immediately spouted some more profanity at her while stuffing her head back between his thighs to finish the job.

Now, as he happened to be bent over at the waist, with this sheep's head stuffed between his thighs, you can probably picture what his backside offered.

Heh...

Of course, I was directly in front of him, so I got a sheep's eye view of what then transpired.

Cousin Genie-bub, who was directly behind Unc Stub, assisting his father, Unc Gene, suddenly got that devilish grin on his face and decided this would be a good time to "goose" Unc Stub.

Oh yeah...I'm talking the ol' "turn your head and cough" sort of goose.

Oh my!

A bellow that could be heard by the neighbors came roaring out of poor ol' Unc Stub, and the look in his eyes of total despair was priceless.

Truly a Kodak moment if there ever was one.

Somehow the sheep and the shears survived, although we were all ducking for cover.

Once Unc figured out what had actually happened, instead of what he thought had happened, he wasn't sure whether to be royally pissed off, or to join the rest of us in belly-splitting laughter.

I told you we were "earthy".

In retrospect, it did serve to lighten the mood, and put all of us in a better frame of mind while we finished up the day's work. Even Stub was laughing about it after he got his bearings back. I figured at some point, some day, when he least expected it, Cuz

Genie-bub was to receive retribution, and I was gleefully anticipating such an adventure. Then, I realized I should be careful what I wished for, because I knew my turn would be coming, too.

That is another story for another day, but this story is still one the favorites to be recounted at events when the men get together away from more sensitive ears.

Story Twenty

Adrift

The old adage is "A farmer works from sunrise to sunset, but a farmer's wife's work is never done." This is a truism for sure. My stories depict the perpetual hard grueling work that being a farmer entails, and hopefully, to some degree, how much work the women of the family were responsible for above and beyond being the grandmother, mother, wife, housekeeper, secretary, nurse, teacher, chef, and general manager. Clearly, it was a true partnership. The women-folk often got little credit for all their work, but we men-folk surely appreciated all they did, every day, with hardly a disparaging word. The women of the family were amazing—hard working, nurturing, humor-filled, tolerant, tough, gritty, beautiful, and tireless.

That is why, on occasion, we men would spend a day off fishing, hunting, or otherwise frolicking. We needed to give these lovely ladies a break from the daily grind. We were chivalrous men, after all.

We would often go off on a two or three day "fishing trip" in the northern climes of Maine, usually Memorial Day weekend. We also would take an afternoon and go ice fishing in the winter months, or go fiddle-heading in the spring. We would forage for ol' Ma Nature's bounty in the late summer/early fall and pick wild blackberries and raspberries. We would dig dandelion greens in the spring. We would hunt in every season. We would go clamming and on occasion, combine fishing in the Belfast Bay with clamming on Islesboro, an island located about three miles east of the Belfast boat landing. That was usually a day-long adventure which was always a ton of fun, and always fruitful. We would enjoy mackerel, bluefish, and striped bass caught while fishing our way to Islesboro, and we would enjoy steamed and/or fried clams dug on Islesboro.

Idyllic.

In the summer of 1970, we embarked on such an adventure. What made this particular adventure especially memorable was the fact that it included two events which made it one we would never forget.

My sister had moved to Kansas to attend the University of Kansas the previous fall, where she met this young man who was from a small town in southwest Kansas. They fell in love, and a few short months later, Sis wrote to tell us she was married. She sent pictures of their wedding, Sis absolutely beautiful in her wedding dress, standing in front of this old Dodge van hand-painted in various psychedelic colors of those days, and adorned with countless peace symbols. Beside her was this young fella with long hair and a scruffy beard.

My family was gathered in my grandmother's living room shortly after the letter and pictures arrived in the mail. My father read the letter to us all and started passing the pictures around for everyone to see. You see, my sister was the first-born of her generation, and was the bona fide princess of the family. She had been crowned "Miss Belfast" her senior year in high school, and then crowned "Maine Broiler Queen" the following summer. She was our princess and her family wanted to check out who this fella was. As the pictures were passed from hand to hand, one uncle after another muttered, "Damn hippie."

My grandmother pointed out, "Well, he has nice teeth."

So anyway, the stage had been set. Now we were waiting for Sis and her new hubby to come home to Maine to see us, and so we could kick the tires on this long-hair and check him out while he still had that new husband smell. She finally found the courage to make the trip to Maine the following spring. They arrived the day before my father and mother were to go to court to be divorced. Steve, her new husband, was assigned the task of sitting with my mother while all those Littlefields were sitting with my father. I was not allowed in the courtroom.

You get the picture.

It took Steve less time than a New York minute to win the hearts of all of us. He turned out to be a man with strong character, solid convictions, and he absolutely adored my sister. He was kind and very bright. His personality was low-keyed and he immediately reminded most of us of my grandfather with his warm and witty sense of humor. He was now a Littlefield.

He and my sister are now the patriarch and matriarch of our family. He will always be my big brother.

They moved in with my mom, and Steve took a job with a carpenter crew rebuilding the Morrill Baptist Church, which had burned flat a few months prior. The plan was to wait 'til I was out of school for the summer, then I would travel with them as they migrated back west, meandering from one campground to another. We had so many adventures traveling west, seeing many historical sites and living the life of wanderers that it would take an entire book to tell all those stories.

So, it was early June and school was almost out, and we would be hitting the dusty trail soon. Before we hit the road for parts unknown, Dad decided he wanted to show Steve how we Littlefields recreated. His friend, George Stewart, owned a 19' Chris Craft pleasure boat we often went fishing in. One Saturday morning George, Dad, Steve, and I unloaded the boat at the boat landing in Belfast, parking the truck and the boat trailer in the adjacent lot. We had fishing poles, clamming hoes and baskets, some cold frosty beverages, a few snacks, and a strong desire to have fun. This was especially exciting for Steve, as he grew up in Kansas and never spent much time in ocean waters.

The day had dawned bright with the sun climbing quickly in the eastern sky. It was seasonally warm, lower 70s, and the bay was absolutely beautiful with its blue/green waters and white-tipped gentle waves. The seagulls milled crazily about overhead, squawking and bitching, waiting for a morsel they could dive bomb for. There were sea ducks and terns riding the swells, the rocked edifice that announced the opening to Belfast harbor that was known as "the monument" loomed ahead, just in front of the clanging bell of the red buoy marker swinging back and forth in the incoming tide. The breeze was redolent with the salty smell of the sea, as we maneuvered around lobster buoys, fishing boats, and pleasure boats on our way towards Islesboro, lurking three miles east. We waved to the fishermen lining the old bridge, and watched as a couple of the bullish-like tugs guttered and growled as they moved into their slips. We noticed two or three sailboats out a few miles on either side of Islesboro, catching the breeze, their sails puffed out and billowing. When we got out beyond Young's Lobster Pound wharf, we started dropping fishing lines over the side. Steve and Dad used light spinning rods to fish for mackerel, baiting the 8-hook strings with chunks of herring, while George and I trolled with diamond jigs for stripers. We made huge circles in the boat swinging from just inside the monument to about a half-mile from Islesboro, hitting schools of mackerel here and there, and occasionally getting a hit from a striper. We chatted and listened to stories of "back in the day" from Dad and George, sipping on cold soda for me, and beer for the men. The day was passing without a care in the world and the biggest issue we had was answering the call of nature, tricky in a small boat.

We stopped in a cove off Islesboro for lunch, George throwing an anchor made of rope and an old tire rim off a semi. Munching sandwiches and feeling pretty relaxed we talked of how we could disperse all the fish we had caught. It wasn't a huge haul, but probably 25 pounds of mackerel and five or six good-sized striped bass. Good eats for sure. We knew the family would be happy to have some fresh fish for dinner the next day.

After lunch, we pulled anchor and puttered around Turtle Head to the north side of the island. We occasionally saw people on shore, hiking, playing, or sunning themselves. We could also see Blue Hill and Castine in the distance on the mainland. As we moved east we finally found the cove we were looking for and put in. George cut the motor about 10' from shore and the boat glided until we could hear the soft scrape of sand and gravel. Steve and I jumped out of the boat, holding a rope tied to the bow and pulled her up on shore as far as we could. We then tied her off to a tree trunk about 50' from shore. George and Dad clambered out of the boat, bringing the clamming hoes and baskets. We also had brought a large kettle, planning on building a fire on shore and steaming up some clams for a nice little mid-afternoon snack.

We hiked around the shore of the cove for a while, checking out the lay of the land, pointing out the indigenous trees of Maine to Steve, and exploring an area on the west side of the cove which had some serious erosion that had left a deep cutout showing many layers of sand, gravel, clay, seaweed, and mounds of clam shells. George told us the mounds of clam shells under 20' of different layers of earth was indicative of an Indian encampment many moons ago. I thought this was pretty cool, and Steve and I dug and kicked around looking for any other sort of artifacts we could find. After an hour of this, and finding nothing to speak of, we decided to get down to clamming.

Dad had taught me that the clams in gravel, while easier to dig, were grittier. So, we always dug in the rocks, rolling them over, pulling the seaweed out of our way, scratching and clawing for the large, sweet, black-shelled clams. It was hard work, but we were in no hurry, taking our time and resting from time to time to have a cold one. After about two hours of digging we all had our clam hods filled and waded out to rinse the clams in the now outgoing tide. The boat now had about 10 feet of terra firma between it and the water's edge. We hadn't paid much attention to the tide, and the waterline was receding rapidly. So, Steve and I were commissioned to scout the woods to find a few blow downs to act as rollers so we could get the boat back afloat. While we were doing this, Dad and George gathered driftwood and some dry pine to build a fire on the shore. Steve and I came out of the woods both dragging a couple of ten-foot long blow downs just as the fire was being started. The four of us managed to get the rollers under the back end of the boat, and with much grunting and sweating, we were finally able to push the ol' girl onto the surf. We gave her another 50' of line so she could ride the outgoing tide without becoming beached again.

We filled the canner half full of clams and added a quart or so of sea water, covered the clams with seaweed and stuck it on the edge of the fire, waiting for the water to come to a boil. We sat on larger chunks of driftwood or rocks and listened to the sounds of the sea, the waves ebbing and flowing, and the gentle whistle of the wind as it passed through the trees just off the beach. The clams were ready soon and we started eating them right out of the canner, shucking them and popping them in our mouths, drinking the champagne in the shells. So caught up in this incredibly peaceful moment we didn't realize how much time had passed until we noticed dusk was falling and the twinkling lights on the shoreline of the mainland seemed to be fading...hmmm.

Fog.

Very heavy, pea soup fog.

It was rolling in quickly. We hurriedly gathered our things, scattered the coals of the fire and extinguished them, hot-footed it to the rope and pulled the boat to the shore and threw our baskets of clams, our kettle, and ourselves into the boat. I was the last aboard as I untied the rope from the tree trunk, ran back and jumped in as we oared ourselves out to deep enough water to drop the motor. The fog continued to roll in, thicker and thicker by the minute. George couldn't get the light torch that stood erect on the back end of the aft side of the boat to work, so while he fiddled with it, the boat spun in lazy circles tethered to the anchor. We lost all sense of direction. My father had a pocket compass, but it was having a hard time convincing him that it was correct. He said it didn't make any sense, to which I reasoned that the compass was right and he was wrong. Dad told me to sit there and shut up. By this time not only was it pitch black dark, it was so foggy I'm pretty sure he couldn't see my one finger salute from four feet away.

You get the...ahem...(a)drift.

We were no more than 25' from shore, but had no idea which way was which. We couldn't see a single landmark, or land for that matter. We couldn't see a light, except the ones on the boat that George finally had working. The fog was so suffocating that we could feel the moisture in the air like a second slimy skin.

Well.

We listened.

Was that the clanging red buoy?

We thought it was, so we putt-putted at less than two knots per hour, stopping to listen every few feet.

We lost the sound of the bell clanging. We were not sure how we managed to lose the sound of that bell. We were starting to think of this as a "situation" rather than an adventure. We did not want to drift out into open ocean. We kept on stopping to listen for sounds every so often, trying to determine if we were going with or against the tide, trying to figure out where the mainland was. Unbelievably, I fell asleep. I awoke when I heard Steve holler. "There...see the light?"

We all squinted and looked in the direction his ghostly finger was pointing. It WAS a light. We pondered what light it might be. George thought it might be the Rockland breakwater. Dad said it might be a ship docked off Searsport. We figured we were on the south side of Islesboro, somewhere between Rockland and Searsport, with Belfast somewhere in between. We started tracking towards the light, praying it didn't disappear. We came closer and closer until we could hear the waves breaking on shore. George cut the motor and we pulled it up and locked it. Using oars, Dad and George paddled us towards shore, while Steve was sprawled across the bow, lying on his belly, head hanging over the edge trying to watch for rocks, while I tried to peer through the fog for any site of land. We finally spotted the shore, and we oared up till the ground was scraping. George jumped out and waded ashore as we noticed a cabin with a porch light glowing dimly through the soup. He knocked on the door loudly a few times. It was midnight by this time. Finally, the door opened and we could hear snippets of conversation as George basically asked, "Where in the name of Christ, are we?"

George waded back to the boat and clambered aboard, telling us the cabin contained a young couple on their honeymoon. Now, that's a story for their future grandchildren eh? Anyway, he said we had come ashore in Lincolnville, and if we took a compass reading we should be able to find our way back to Belfast now that we had our bearings. So, we took a reading and with Dad acting as navigator George attempted to pilot us back to the landing in Belfast.

We missed.

Not by a whole lot really, but we missed. We did, however, see another light, which we made a bee-line for. It turned out to be the large tanker ship docked at Searsport. As we idled up to it, I thought it looked like a floating skyscraper. It was a really big ship. We could see a few people milling about on deck, which seemed some 100' above us. We hollered, they hollered. We hollered again, they hollered back again. The problem was, we hollered in English, they hollered in what we believed was Russian. So, after a few minutes of international detente, we waved good-bye to our new friends and decided to follow the shoreline back to Belfast. The fog was thinning a bit at this time, but between it and the darkness it was still a little tricky navigating. So, Steve once again took his radar-like position sprawled on the bow of the boat, ever watchful for impediments like those nasty rocks I mentioned earlier. Dad popped open a beer, took a swig, belched and said, "Well, this has been fun." George may have giggled, we were having a shitload of fun. I shucked a few clams and ate them raw, hey, a boy needs to keep up his strength.

It was nearing daylight when we saw the ghostly outline of the new bridge crossing Belfast bay. We finally spied the landing and idled to it, me jumping out and securing the boat to the wharf. As the rest of the crew departed the boat, we noticed a Coast Guard cutter docked and one of the uniformed young men stepped up the metal gangway and asked our names. He said they had been called by a Debbie Bird about 11:00 p.m. last night fearing the worst.

Yikes!

Remember folks, no cell phones in those days, and with that fog, smoke signals wasn't gonna cut it.

Steve went to the pay phone located on the side of the harbormaster's shack and called his still blushing bride. She was not happy. Steve was getting an earful, and I just knew it wasn't going to stop there.

Dad and George chatted with the CG seaman and told him what had transpired. He issued the usual lectures, but stopped when he realized these two guys had at least 20 years on him and they weren't about to listen to much from a whippersnapper like him. So, he grinned ruefully and wished us luck when we got home to our family.

Heh.

We figured we had fish and clams to soften the blow of scaring the ever living beJesus out of our family.

Sis wasn't having any of it. She figured she'd earned the right to blister all of us with a finger shaking, sharp-tongued, lecture that would make a porn star blush.

"My husband, make that my NEW husband, my father, and my brother, all lost at sea!!! You wonder why I didn't want to come home!"

Well, it was a while before Sis would get over that one. Eventually she did allow us all to play together again, and we have had many adventures since. Some of those adventures included Sis, who wasn't afraid of a little exploring either. In fact, the next year, she gave birth to my niece who has got the itch for adventure like the rest of us.

My stories have now become generational to include the next generation, or perhaps that generation will produce a storyteller or two of their own.

Story Twenty-One

The Donkey, the Mailbox, and the Tree Trail

Growing up on a farm allows a young fella with an active imagination lots of opportunities to make his elders shake their heads and wonder "just what ta hell was you thinking?!"

Seems I may have caused my fair share of these sort of moments, and one could say I had even developed, among my elders, something of a reputation, or as I preferred to think of it, "farm-cred".

Yes, I was adept at taking the most placid of situations and jacking them up to an all hands on deck, full scale rescue deployment.

It's a gift.

So anyway, on this farm he had a duck, ee i, ee i, o.

Actually we did have ducks, geese, pigs, sheep, cows, goats, horses, a mule, and a donkey. Uh…ee i, ee i, o.

This story is about the donkey. The donkey was named Ed Muskie, after our native political son. I don't recall where we got ol' Ed, or even when, it seems he was always there from the time I started remembering stuff, and stayed around until I was in high school. About then Unc Gene donated him to Camp Fair Haven for the kids to play with while on their summer vacation on the shores of Randall Pond.

We also had a mule named Ginny, but she ain't in this story.

I mention her because there is a difference between mules and donkeys.

Wikipedia tells us:

"A male donkey or ass is called a jack, a female a jenny or jennet; a young donkey is a foal. Jack donkeys are often used to mate with female horses to produce mules. A mule is the offspring of a male donkey (jack) and a female horse (mare). It has been claimed that mules are "more patient, sure-footed, hardy and long-lived than horses, and they are considered less obstinate, faster, and more intelligent than donkeys."

I don't know about the "more intelligent" part. Ginny was pretty smart, but ol' Ed had a little something between those long floppy ears, too. He sure as hell was stubborn, and he was the worst damned ride I've ever had. All hurky-jerky, like riding a cow.

It's important to note that Ed loved two things more than anything else.

One, he loved cigarettes. He'd eat 'em and ask for more, cigarettes became sort of a featured snack for Ed.

Two, he loved green grass, the longer the better. Like the stuff that grows around fence posts or mailbox posts, that the lawnmower can't get to.

One summer day, Cuz Genie-Bub and I were dawdling around in the pasture across the road from his house. We played a game or two of horseshoes, then climbed the golden delicious apple tree and had a snack, and then we contemplated going down to the brook to see if we could catch a trout or two. I figured that I would come out on the losing end of the fish competition as I always did. Cuz was a great fisherman, patient and skilled at leading his line so it wouldn't snag in the alders and blow downs that congested the brook. He said that was where the best trout were found because they liked the shade. Conversely, I hadn't discovered patience at this point in my life, and I wasn't particularly skilled at anything to do with fishing, except get my line and worm snagged in the blow downs and alders. So, I figured that since I was gonna lose that race, I might as well use my superior size to push Cuz down in a cow flap, jump over him, and hop on ol' Ed, who just happened to be hanging around hopeful for a ciggy-snack. Cuz and I were the same age, and although we were first cousins, his dad being my dad's older brother, we were more like brothers since we spent most all of our time together. Genie-Bub was the quiet dutiful son who paid attention when the elders tried to impart a life or farm lesson, while yours truly usually had his head in the clouds. This meant, even though I often caused my elders to heave huge sighs, sometimes it was a matter of being framed by the oh so dutiful one. He was clever about it, and had perfected the innocent look, I didn't stand a chance. So, I took my shots when an opportunity presented itself.

Now, as I mentioned, ol' Ed was a horrible ride, but I decided riding Ed and making Cuz walk to the creek was preferable to the other way around. He was too small for both of us to ride, and as I mentioned, he was stubborn as a...well...mule...even though he was a donkey. I didn't have a cigarette to bribe the ol' boy with, and it was apparent that Ed had decided, "no snack, no ride." He dug his front hooves in and refused to move. Genie-Bub went over to the roadside gate where the grass was long and green around the posts and pulled some, waving it at Ed, who decided he would hurk and jerk over for a nibble of what Cuz was offering. Cuz said, "I'll feed him this grass and you start putting your heels to him and pull on his mane, that'll make him head towards the creek...don't worry, I'll catch up to ya."

I thought this was pretty neighborly of Cuz, especially after I pushed him down in a cow flap to get to Ed first. So, I took his advice and started kicking my heels into Ed's ribs about the time he was munching on the green grass. Good ol' Cuz with a gleam in his eye, opened the gate to freedom and beyond. Ed, realizing this, decided all of a sudden it was time to take off like he'd been shot in the ass (pun intended), through the gate and down the road.

Cuz told me afterwards it was quite a sight to see. Ol' Ed with his discombobulated lurch pounding down the road, with a wide-eyed eight-year-old boy looking like one of those bobble-head figurines one gets at a ballgame, hanging onto his mane for all he's worth, moving further down the road with every bone-jarring thump of his front hooves.

Payback is a bitch.

After Ed and I did this hurk-jerk dance for about 100 yards we came upon the Floods' house, which was the next place down the road from Unc Gene's. The Floods were also family, but on my mother's side. Aunt Bea was my mom's older sister and she lived there with her husband, her four boys, and her daughter. Aunt Bea was a sweet lady who always loved to see me and she was the author of my nickname, which some family members continue to call me to this day.

Mitchy-boo.

Very masculine, eh?

Anyway, ol' Ed, as he is trying to run out from under me, spies the Floods' mailbox. More precisely, he spies all that lovely long iridescent green grass growing around the mailbox post, and he made the split second decision to stop, put his head down, and chow on the aforementioned grass.

And, I mean stop, like right now.

Yes, Ed stopped, I didn't.

It flashed through my mind at that moment that the cow patty I pushed Cuz into didn't hurt half as much as the mailbox post I found myself piled up against did.

It hurt my pride more than anything else, especially when I picked myself up to the sound of laughter. I peered around, I couldn't see anyone, but I could hear four voices laughing and twittering at me.

Ed, meanwhile, seemed quite pleased with himself. He munched away, peering at me sideways from time to time.

Then I hear, "Mitchell-boo, look up here."

I followed the sound with my eyes until I spied my cousin Terry, the oldest of the four boys, waving at me from about 15 feet up in a tree on the edge of the woods in his yard. Everyone in that family called me Mitchy-boo, except Terry, who called me Mitchell-boo. I supposed it seemed more formal somehow.

Then I hear, "How'd you like kissing that post?" from Ronny, the next oldest, waving from another tree.

Johnny and Jeff, rounding out the fearsome-foursome, were grinning like a dog with a mouth full of bumblebees from yet two other trees. They were all having a great time at my expense, albeit 15 feet off the ground.

I queried, "Any of you boys ever fall from a tree?"

This brought another round of raucous laughter. "Catch us if you can!" hollered Jeff, and they started moving.

I watched in amazement as these four cousins of mine started moving through the trees like monkeys in a rain forest. From tree to tree, all around their property, never touching the ground. I realized by watching them, that the three boys behind Terry mimicked his movements from branch to branch, tree to tree. They had developed a tree-trail that ranged from a mere eight feet to as high as 20, but never did they touch the ground, or fall. This was the epitome of cool. I wanted to do it.

I glanced at Ed, who seemed content to mow the lawn, and figured he'd be ok for a while. After all, it wasn't fair that I spend all my time with my father's side of the family, I was needed here on my mom's side of the tracks, right?

I scrambled up a tree and figured to catch up, only to become stumped. How the heck did they do this? I decided that if they could do it, I could too, so I took a leap of faith, literally, and jumped from the maple I had climbed to grab a limb on a nearby cedar. I managed to get my hands on the cedar bough, but my weight brought me back down to the ground in a heap.

More laughter.

This was stacking up to be one of those days.

As I sat there nursing my wounded pride I noticed something missing…

Ed had sauntered off. Then I heard a horn blaring.

Uh oh.

At least this brought the boys out of the trees to see the action taking place down the road. Ol' Ed had decided he had gone as far as he wanted and stood smack dab in the middle of the road, blocking traffic. He wasn't gonna move either. I looked back towards Unc Gene's to see Cuz and Unc walking my way as the Flood boys and I headed down the road to see if we could entice Ed to move out of the road and let people, and vehicles, to pass by.

It became something of a cluster, me and Ed surrounded by several motorists looking a might peeved, the Flood boys standing around highly amused, and Unc and Genie-bub finally making the party complete. Unc looked at me, shook his head, pulled a Pall Mall out of his pocket as an enticement to get Ed to the side of the road. Ed looked serene as he chewed up the cigarette. We all walked back to the farm, with ol' Ed acting like a choir boy all of a sudden. I think he'd had enough adventure and wanted back in the confines of the pasture where it was safe and there were no blaring horns. Genie-bub was smirking, the Flood boys were laughing it up, and Unc Gene was still shaking his head. I figured I was gonna hear it from Dad later, and I knew pleading my case of being framed by Cuz wasn't gonna cut it. So, I begged another Pall Mall off Unc, fed it to Ed, and thanked him for such a fun ride as we closed the gate with the donkey inside.

As we walked back to his house, Unc patted me on the back, nodded at Genie-bub and said, "You know boys, ol' Ed here got more sense than either of you do."…but he was smiling as he said it.

Story Twenty-Two

The Drive-In Movies

I was born in the mid-50s, so I grew up in the 60s and graduated from high school in the early 70s. My sister was born seven years before me, and so got a jump start on the cultural and social revolution our generation was experiencing during that period of time. Needless to say there was a slight "rift" between our generation and our parents' culture that kept things interesting. My sister was wise enough to realize that the 60s generation with its wild psychedelic music, bell-bottom jeans, leather sandals, peace signs, long-haired bearded men, peace marches, pot smoking, pill popping, and general overall counter-culture ways would never be tolerated by Dad and the Uncs back on the farm, in little ol' 'Podunk' Maine, where inside toilets were still a new and exciting creation. So, she did what most kids of that era did to get away from the oppression of her family, she went off to college.

Me? I stayed on the farm, determined to fight the good fight of my generation, to bring these rednecks into the world of enlightenment, to show them the beauty of world peace and how it could be obtained, if we all just 'chilled out' and made love instead of war. I figured if I grew my hair long, listened to that hippie music, stayed drunk and stoned a majority of the time, and preached of the wisdom of George McGovern that Dad and the Uncs would see how far advanced our generation was, and they would naturally fall in line.

Dad always said that Sis was the smarter one.

For me it was a bit of a paradox. While I cherished my heritage, loved the way of life and work that a family farm has to offer, thought my grandfather was a God, and wanted to mimic my Dad and Uncs' every move and every word, I was drawn to the eye-opening excitement and energy that the world outside of Belfast, Maine, offered in general, and the message of "we can change the world" that the 60s generation held in particular. So, I tried to learn both, do both, and be both.

Sort of like learning French and English at the same time, I never was sure of which world I belonged in.

For a while, during high school and after, but before I got married, I moved between both worlds. I spent the summers with my sister and her new husband. One summer I spent in Philadelphia where they worked and lived. I have to tell you, going from the family farm in Belfast, Maine, to Philadelphia, Pennsylvania, is one hell of an experience for a 14-year-old farm boy. The following summer Sis and Steve moved from Philly back to Maine and hung out until I was out of school, at which time we packed all their belongings, including the old Ted Williams canvas tent Dad had, into a U-Haul, and hooked it onto the aged Volvo they drove, and struck off cross country. Once again, what an adventure! Then, shortly after high school, I moved to Colorado and lived with them for a period of time.

All of these adventures would culminate in me going back to Maine…back to the farm…back to the world of Pup, Dad, and the Uncs. I guess you could say that I had the best of both worlds.

Until.

Until Sis became one of them.

Yes, one of them. She moved back to Maine, bought a farm up in the county, and started having kids. She started teaching school!! Worse, she also taught Sunday school, for Christ sakes. As if that wasn't bad enough, her husband, Steve, became an accountant. They said it was respectable…ppfffftttt!!

Radical counter-culture 60s hippies my ass!

Anyway, I had to plot my revenge.

First, I got married, then I got a full-time job, and then I decided it was time for a trip to the county and a visit to Sis and Steve. So we made plans for Susie, my wife, and me to spend a weekend with Sis and Steve at their farm in Ft. Fairfield, Maine.

We arrived that Friday night to a few drinks, supper and then a stroll around the beautiful farm and lands they called home, overlooking the sparkling river, and surrounded by beautiful forests of green.

The next morning dawned bright and clear and I put my plan into action. I went to town with Steve to pick up a few things which I would need for the coming evening—a half gallon of 110 proof vodka and a gallon of milk. Once back at their farm I proceeded to show them the art of making coffee brandy. We first brewed some coffee, extra strong, then took the half gallon of 110 proof vodka and put half of that into another bottle. Next we added about a pint of the very strong coffee to each of the bottles of vodka and finished it off with a healthy dollop or two of vanilla extract to each bottle. Then we stuck them in the fridge to cool and "age". Then I talked my sister into going to the local drive-in movies that evening. It was a Bond flick showing. I told her we would go in my car so no one would recognize her.

So, evening comes, it's Saturday night in Ft. Fairfield, Maine, uh-wooo-hooo! The four of us pile into my old '68 Chevy Impala and head off to the drive-in movies in Presque Isle, about 10 miles away. In the car are the two bottles of now aged coffee brandy along with a cooler filled with ice and the gallon of milk. I had packed some plastic cups and we took various snacks, bags of chips, cookies, etc. After we pull into the drive-in and find a good spot, we settle in for the movie and I break out the refreshments. Of course, Sis, who is all respectable now, is nervously looking around to see if anyone sees her. I assure her that a little drinky-poo will help her relax and enjoy the movie. Apparently, it took several drinks for her to relax, because before long Sis appeared quite relaxed indeed, and one of the bottles of coffee brandy was gone. I figured that was my cue to dig out my trusty bag of pot and roll a joint.

Yes, the night was getting interesting.

My sister, while holding a drink in one hand and the joint in the other, tried her very best to scold me about the dangers of drinking too much and that pot was illegal. It was sort of cute the way she slurred her words and shook her finger at me while she was holding the joint. I told her that I was going to mend my ways as soon as the other bottle was gone, and the bag of pot we were smoking was gone. Sis, being the good older sister that she was, decided that the sooner that stuff was gone, the quicker I could start on the path of redemption. So she helped me finish both the bag and the bottle. Fortunately, Susie didn't drink, so we had a sober person to drive us, hooting and hollering, and singing all the way home from the drive-in movies to the farm. Once back at her farm, we discovered that Sis's legs wouldn't work. So, being the dutiful brother that I am, I helped Steve carry her up the stairs to their bedroom.

The next morning, Sunday, Susie and I get up and decide to pack up and hit the road early as it's a four-hour drive back to Belfast. As she packed our bag I went downstairs to inform Sis and Steve that we would be leaving early to get back before dark, and I found Steve sitting at the kitchen table with a cup of steaming coffee. I poured myself one and sat down and asked, "Where's Sis?"

He grinned, "Well, she's gotta teach Sunday school in about an hour. I think she is out on the porch going over her lesson."

I got up and walked out to the enclosed porch and there I found Sis, dressed in her Sunday best, lying on a chaise lounge, with a cold washcloth over her brow, her lesson lying on her stomach, and she was groaning.

I remarked, "Gee, Sis, you look like you don't feel so hot."

She informed me that I was despicable. She managed to do this without moving a muscle through clenched teeth. I was impressed. So, I took her washcloth and went into the kitchen and ran it under cold water and wrung it out and took it back and laid it back on her brow. I told her, "Well, Sis, Susie and I are gonna leave so we can get back to Belfast at a reasonable hour. Had a ball, thanks for having us, enjoy Sunday school, love ya."

Her reply was short and sweet, four words actually, once again delivered without moving any muscles and through clenched teeth, and highlighted with a moan.

"Don't. Ever. Come. Back."

Of course, I've gone back countless times, and we have had many more adventures, including the time we kept calling everyone we knew after midnight one New Year's Eve, and playing Auld Lang Syne on homemade kazoos. But never again has Sis drank homemade coffee brandy or gone to a drive-in movie with me. I have no idea why.

Story Twenty-Three

Smile

When I decided that I needed to write this story, a tribute really, about a man who was, and still is, such a big influence on everyone who knew him, I recognized that I have always identified the song "Smile" with this man.

The song, of course, has become an American standard, and has been sung by many over the years. Most people are surprised to learn that the music to this favorite was written by the legendary silent film star Charlie Chaplin.

He composed the song to be used as the theme to one of his very last and ultimately one of the best known silent films, Modern Times, released in 1936.

The song didn't become known as "Smile" until lyrics were added in 1954 by John Turner and Geoffrey Parsons and it was recorded by Nat King Cole. It reached #10 on the Billboard charts that same year.

Ahhhh, ol' Nat, now that was a man with such an incredible voice. I never tire of listening to him croon.

Another man who could "sing a little" was David.

No last name needed, just David. Anyone who knew him, knows who this story is about. Most of you probably figured it out by the title of the song and the title to this story.

Actually he had a few monikers, David, Dave, Bach, depending on who was talking to him, or about him. David is easily identified by this song because among his many gifts, he possessed a million mega-watt smile.

Really, he did.

The man could light up a room with that damn smile and he always, always, did.

That damn smile was ever-present, and typically it was accompanied by a song. I mentioned the man could "sing a little", didn't I?

For me, David was always a role model and mentor through the years, first as an older cousin when I was young, and then as my supervisor when I was in my twenties as we worked for the same insurance agency. Though our time together was somewhat limited when I was a youngster, when we did see each other David always had the time and patience for his hyper-active, somewhat goofy little cousin. He always made me feel like I was special, that I was important. When we worked together later in life, I realized that David made everyone he spoke to feel special and important.

Million megawatt smile, can sing a little, makes everyone around him feel special, beat that! Hell, I know I can't.

The man exuded a lust for life and a love of people that still remains a benchmark of sorts for me. I figure if I can mimic David, even a little bit, then I can, to some degree, experience the pleasure of life that seemed to come so naturally for him.

Some of you might say, "Well, yeah, here's this guy with all these natural talents. Athletic and popular in his high school days, he was the driving force in a musical band when he was a teenager, possessed tons of charm and charisma, went on to become very successful as an insurance agent in his home town, married a local beauty, had three wonderful kids, why in hell wouldn't he be smiling all the damn time?"

Good point. I guess most of us would be smiling a lot, too, except life is never that easy, or that pure.

Life kicks all of us in the ass, sometimes even guys like David.

Maybe life kicks those guys in the ass even harder than the rest of us.

I do know that David had his share of struggles in life as we all do, including his final battle with a brain tumor that cut his life far too short, but he never, ever stopped with that damn smile. He never lost his love of people, nor his lust for life. He never, to my knowledge, ever compromised his integrity, never felt that he was "a victim", or that he deserved better. No crying in his cups, no anger or petulance, no seeking of sympathy.

In fact, quite the opposite.

He continued to be the supportive friend and father, continued to encourage his children to chase their dreams, and to help them realize to never give up. He continued to be a friend, a confidant, and a mentor to many of his friends, me included.

I recall not long before he died, David was living in town and being closely monitored by two of his sisters. He was in the final stages of his battle with the merciless cancer in his head, and, it was decided that he could not be left alone for any length of time. My wife, Bonnie, and I stopped at the post office to gather our mail and I saw that damn smile approaching us as we were walking into the building. He, of course, grabbed Bonnie in a big hug and kiss, while he flashed that damn smile and winked at me. Then it was my turn for a hug.

"David, how are you doing?"

"If I were any better, I'd be twins."...even bigger smile.

"So, what are you doing? Out for a walk?"

David laughed, "I am trying to stay two steps ahead of my sisters." Another infectious smile.

"Can we give you a ride?"

His eyes twinkled and he kicked that damn smile up to a million-and-a-half megawatts, "Nah...I figure they'll catch up to me in a few minutes, so I'm gonna get as far as I can." With a final wink and his finger on his lips indicating "shhh, this is our secret", he was off and flashing that damn smile as he strolled down Main Street.

It was the last time Bonnie and I saw him.

Bittersweet to be sure.

His refusal to relinquish his independence, and his absolute conviction to maintain his lust for life and love of people, even when he knew his time was all but up, continue to leave an undeniable impression on both of us.

Years earlier, when we were working together, we both belonged to the Lions Club. We were responsible for the "beverage and entertainment" portion of the meetings. This meant that we would go an hour before the other Lions would show up and set up the bar and prepare for the festivities. Usually, we would also stay a half hour or so after the meeting broke up to clean up.

At that time in my life, I was going through a divorce from my first wife, Susie, and I was everything that David never seemed to be—depressed, feeling sorry for myself, angry, petulant, and thinking that I was a victim. "Damn it! This is just so damned unfair!"

So, that night after everyone had left, and David and I were cleaning the hall and putting away chairs, he told me, "Mitch, it's time you stopped with the cry-baby act and move on."

I was a little shocked. He had never spoken to me that way before. I asked him what he meant.

He flashed that damn smile and said, "You know a hundred years from now there is going to be at least a million Chinese that just don't give a shit about your divorce."

I stood there blinking and thinking that over, and then I started to laugh. He was right.

He chucked me in the shoulder and sat at the piano and he started playing. He sang to me in that beautiful voice of his, Chaplin's wonderful song.

Since that night, whenever I hear that song, or when I sing it myself, which is almost daily, I always think of David. Of course, my rendition is nothing like David's, or Nat's, but hey, I love singing that song!

Today, as I write this story, I am once again going through a divorce. It is sad to be sure, but I continue to sing that song, and I continue to remember that damn smile and all that it meant to me, and will always mean to me.

I too, have that lust for life and that love of people, and look forward to every adventure this life has to offer.

Wish that damn smile was still around...

Story Twenty-Four

I'll Sing If I Want To

As in most of my stories I start this one explaining that I grew up on a farm. I suppose it is important to me to make this impression whether or not that fact is germane to the story, because growing up on those three family farms truly has defined my perspective, my sense of humor, and most certainly, my outlook on life in general. So, it is important, I think, to keep this in mind as I write my stories, and, equally important that the reader takes this into account. My life growing up on these farms was, in many respects, a complete contrast to my life since…THAT boy, growing up with THAT family, on THOSE farms, is what I always retreat to, what I cling to, what I believe has enabled me to negotiate the peaks and valleys of life and remain what I've always been…a simple farm boy who loves life and the people in it. A boy who seeks the humor in life and appreciates the natural yin and yang of the universe. As comedian Ron White points out, "You can't fix stupid", and as my grandfather told me, "Ain't none of us getting out of this alive", I figure I might as well spend as much time as possible enjoying this ride and not waste time with what is out of my control.

Growing up on a farm lends itself to a somewhat "earthy" existence. Caring for a mixture of horses, cows, sheep, chickens, ducks, goats, and the occasional tamed crow, one becomes adept at taking the life cycle of these animals in stride and seeing first hand all the aspects of life and how these creatures interact with one another. You might be surprised at how similar this is to our own journey. I haven't quite figured out if the animals are mimicking us, or if it is the other way around.

So, this little story has little to do with my farm boy upbringing except to point out the contrast between the social aspects of different worlds, and how a group of people from a variety of these worlds react when something unexpected happens.

Hang on...I think you're gonna like this one.

In one of my several (so far) incarnations in life, when I was in my early twenties, I left the farm behind and took a job selling liquor for the State. Well now, this was a little different than life with Mamie and Pup. It became quickly apparent to me that I needed to get up to speed with things like social graces and to realize that life and people off the farm were...well...a little more complex. On the other hand, being a liquor store clerk afforded me the opportunity to intermingle with, and study the human condition of, just about every citizen and walk of life our community had to offer.

Heh...most on a fairly regular basis.

From the power brokers to the less fortunate, I serviced them all—got to know some of the more intimate details of their lives and their habits. Amazingly, at the end of the day I found little difference in any of them. However, their personal perspectives regarding our community and the people within were something to behold. From the body language, the attitude, the "whispered asides", to the outright commentary, I saw and heard it all.

Much like the bartender, the barber, or the hairdresser, the liquor store clerk somehow, quite inexplicably, becomes a confidant of sorts for his customers. And, of course, it was implied that anything said or done whilst within the sacred halls of the liquor store was to remain strictly confidential. So, in the spirit of what happens in Vegas, stays in Vegas, I will never divulge names...heh...but I will tell my stories.

So, at the ripe old age of twenty-three I became the manager of this liquor store, which meant that I spent most of my time administering the operations, ordering product and supplies, filling out time sheets and doing payroll, creating work schedules, general accounting of the loot, and running to the bank to deposit all that hard-earned cash.

It was incredibly boring. At least as a clerk I got to see the pulse of the community from an interesting angle, but I needed to make a change. I was going to dry up and die as a liquor store administrator...ugh! I decided my next foray into the world of business should be something a little more dynamic. So I became a life insurance agent.

Yes, one of "those".

I did quite well, too. I worked hard, built an ever-growing clientele, and became involved with several civic organizations within the community. I was making a name for myself and making a decent income as I worked on building my budding career. People took notice. I was becoming one of the "in" people. I got invited to all the holiday parties and business community events, and I was recruited by several businesses as they thought I was "a young man with a strong upside and solid potential."

Heh....right.

I was approached by an insurance agency and I interviewed with them several times. I thought this was an incredible opportunity for me. I was still in my twenties, and I might have the chance at a once-in-a-lifetime job. This agency was pretty good sized, had offices in eight communities, and offered not only a salary plus commission, but an expense account, a brand new company car, a full support staff, an office of my own with nice furniture, AND...I would be working under the tutelage of my cousin.

I mean...WOW! A chance to really move up in the world, and work with someone I loved and respected. I was as happy as I could ever remember being. The farm became a bit of a distant memory. My cousin David was managing the Belfast branch of this insurance agency and he was quick to welcome me with open arms, show me the ropes, give me advice and training, and we became closer than ever. David became a mentor. He tried to instill in me the more refined aspects of life as a member of the business community, and he also was always available with "life in general" advice. This lasted for the rest of his life. I miss him and think of him every day. He reinforced in me the ability to not take myself or this life too seriously—in the end we are all the same.

While David and I worked together, he celebrated his 40th birthday. It was to be a huge celebration with almost the entire community invited to join in the festivities. The local restaurant, Jed's, was employed as the setting for this "don't miss" event, as it contained a banquet/bar/stage area in the back that could be closed off from the rest of the dining area of the building.

Perfect!

Plenty of room for everyone and for all the food and presents....and an operating bar!

Yowser!

All the beautiful people were there, it was the social event of the season. Everyone was mingling, setting their presents to David on the table provided, snagging a few finger-rolls, grabbing a beverage of their choice from the bar. Lots of stories, jokes and innuendos...everyone was laughing it up and having a glorious time. At some point the obligatory birthday "boob" cake, complete with strategically placed candles, was unveiled amid much laughter and many comments. Just as David leaned over and took a bite, face first, of one of the...ahem...boobs on the cake, and as the place erupted in applause and laughter, Tommy Bailey, the bartender, reminded us that there were somewhere around 100 people in the main dining room, and that we should probably bring it down a notch or two. It was, after all, 5:00 on a Saturday afternoon.

We got the message and tried to tone it down a bit.

In this back area, this banquet/bar/stage area, was indeed a stage and dance floor. This was the area where at night local bands would come and play for all of us night-owls who wanted to shake a leg and party the night away. Usually they would begin to play at 9:00 p.m. and continue to entertain until 1:00 a.m., at which time Tommy would gently kick all our asses out. Anyway, this stage area on this afternoon was completely set up with the band's equipment, as they would be playing that evening. We were told to not touch anything or go near the stage or equipment. Mostly we complied.

A few things about David before I proceed.

David possessed a natural charm and grace. He exuded a lust for life and love of people that I continue to admire. He loved to laugh, and he loved to make people laugh along with him. He had a smile that I described as a million megawatts—he lit up rooms with that smile. The man also had another gift. He could sing. David was very talented musically, was the driving force in a musical band in his late teens/early twenties, and for years after would play at local establishments. He was well known for his beautiful voice.

He LOVED to sing, and we loved to hear him do so.

So, after the raucousness of "boob-cake" the crowd once again mingled about, chatting, and enjoying the party. By this time, our birthday boy had enjoyed a few gifts from the bar and was grinning that grin of the alcoholically enlightened.

I just knew something was gonna happen...

David, in his enlightened condition, decided it was time he did what he loved to do so much—sing.

And, since there happened to be a stage available, he figured that would be the place to do this singing, and hey!, whaddyaknow-lookie there, why there's a microphone sitting in its stand right there on center stage.

David, with that million megawatt smile on full high beam bounded onto the stage, grabbed the mic and starts belting out Elvis's rendition of "It's Now or Never". The crowd loved it...his wife did not. She ran to the stage and grabbed his arm, "David, David, you have to stop, you are embarrassing me!"

To which David replied, "It's my fucking birthday. I'll sing if I want to," with that shit-eating grin on his face.

I'm pretty sure David did not realize that when he grabbed the mic, he inadvertently hit the button to turn it on, and, not only was his singing and his and his wife's charming little exchange heard through the band's speakers, but it was heard throughout the entire restaurant's PA system.

"Today's specials include a mix of contemporary marital bliss, infused with some risqué commentary, and finished lovingly with a charmingly drunken version of a famous standard. Would you mind a heaping helping of this along with your fried clams today, folks?" might be what the waitresses were saying to the amused diners out in the other part of the restaurant.

I was literally rolling on the floor along with Tommy the bartender and a few of the other guys. Some of the ladies were covering their mouths and of course a few people pretended to be indignant.

David did what he always did—took it all in stride, grinned that grin, and finished singing the song.

Ahhhh...life. You gotta love it.

Story Twenty-Five

Epilogue/The Fox

So, we come to the end of this book. I can't express my appreciation enough to all those who have helped me make this book possible, and make it a reality. Especially you readers. You have honored me by reading my stories, and by extension, assisted me in keeping the legacy of an enchanted lifestyle, and incredible family alive.

I have so many of these stories running around in my head. I intend to continue writing these stories for as long as I am able to sit at the keyboard and let these memories and fantasies take on life of their own. I have been writing stories since I was in the 7th grade, some 46 years ago. Unfortunately, many of those stories, written by hand on legal pads, have been lost through time. In the mid 90s, when most of us discovered the new and fantastic world of computers and the internet, I was able to store my stories as I wrote them. Also, I found sitting at the keyboard much easier than writing by hand. The stories seemed to flow easier, and it is certainly much easier to read my words and make corrections or change the flow of the story. Many of the stories contained within this book are stories that were written from those days when I first sat at a keyboard and let it take on a life of its own. Some are new.

What I have begun to think about is all the lost stories. I think that over that period of time, there were instances when I would have a fit of inspiration, fueled by a memory or a story being told to me by an elder, that produced a story that I wish I had been able to preserve. So, I am picking my own memory of some of those stories and trying to re-create them. At least the ones I remember. I often stop in the middle of a conversation, or while driving my car, and scribble a memory flash on a piece of scrap paper, so I don't forget it, and can try to turn that into either a re-creation of a story I've written in the past, or a story yet to be told.

It is a process. Sometimes these little fits of inspiration bring eye rolling and/or strange looks from whomever I happen to be with at the time. My family is used to it. Usually they just sigh and wait for me to get re-involved in the current discussion. Thanks for humoring me, guys.

All the stories in this book to this point are based on my own memories or stories told to me. That is to say, these stories are factual. They happened. Of course, like anyone who writes stories, I have taken a bit of literary license here or there to help with the flow and/or the content of the story, but the stories are real.

So now, I am going to tell you a story that is factual, followed by a completely fictitious story. They sort of go together. This factual story will explain how an eleven-year-old farm boy caught the writing bug. Where it all began.

***

When I entered the sixth grade at the George Robinson School in Belfast, Maine, in the 1967-1968 school year, it was the first time I experienced multiple teachers and multiple classrooms. So, the sixth grade was something to look forward to. It meant we were no longer considered "little kids", we were fledgling adults that needed to expand our knowledge by attending a different classroom, with a different teacher, for each subject we were studying.

One such teacher was Miss Farley. Miss Farley taught sixth grade English, and at first blush probably figured this somewhat hyper farm boy was going to be a challenge. She was stern. She often would admonish me for speaking out of turn, or telling jokes to my classmates, and for generally not paying attention. I mean c'mon, it was English—my first (and only) language—what did I need to pay attention for? I knew how to speak English just fine. In fact she often pointed out to me in front of the entire class that I over-used the English language consistently.

Seemed a little confusing to me.

After a few detentions, where I was not allowed to join my classmates outside for recess, I started to see things her way a little more.

Anyway, as the school year proceeded she introduced the class to some of the classics, and I got hooked on the adventures contained within the pages of these tomes. I had become a voracious reader by the time I was nine years old, burning through all 56 Hardy Boys mysteries in less than a year. Nancy Drew, the Alfred Hitchcock Little Detectives series, anything that offered adventure, I would read and sometimes re-read. It seemed I couldn't get enough. My parents and my older sister would take me to Palmer's Stationery, in town, to grab two or three new books each week. Bless them. We could hardly afford it, I'm sure, but the burning desire to read these adventures on my part, and the fact that it kept me quiet and out of mischief, on theirs, made it a worthwhile investment.

Of course, I wasn't the only one. Many of my classmates had the same itch to read these stories that Miss Farley was introducing us to. *Moby Dick, Robinson Crusoe, Gulliver's Travels, Tom Jones, Little Women, Huckleberry Finn, The Call of the Wild, Catch-22,* and my personal favorite, *The Catcher in the Rye,* fed my imagination and to this day, has me ever craving more.

Then one day, Miss Farley, that wonderful nurturing woman that made such a huge impact on me and my classmates, threw me a curve ball. Right out of the blue.

She told the class one Friday, "Starting Monday, each of you will have a half hour of class each day throughout the week to write your own story. You all should think about this over the weekend. It is a week-long project for each of you, and your story must be on my desk, completed, by the following Monday."

I thought, "What???!!...write a story??...why??...what's wrong with reading stories? I like reading stories, why do I have to write a story???"

I said, "About what?"

She reminded me that I should raise my hand and be called on before I blurted out what everyone was thinking, and added, "Whatever you would like to write about."

Hrumph. Like that helped.

So, since it was Friday, and I had a whole week before I had to worry about this damn story, I didn't bother to think about it. Ha!

The following week, each day in class, while my classmates were sitting there, many with their tongues protruding out of the corner of their mouths, deep in thought as they labored over their stories, I sat there and day-dreamed about all the adventures I'd have later that day on the farm—when I got out of this prison. Oh, I had a pad of paper in front of me, and I'd occasionally make a show of deep thought and scribbling, even occasionally sticking my own tongue out of the corner of my mouth, mimicking my classmates, when Miss Farley looked my way, but the story was not coming along very well.

The week passed, and on Friday, Miss Farley reminded us that our stories were to be completed and put on her desk when we entered the classroom the following Monday. I figured, "What the heck, I can do this sometime over the weekend."

Heh, uh huh, sure.

The weekend was filled with adventure for me. We did our usual chores about the farms, and then went ice fishing on Saturday at Cross Pond. I always loved eating hot dogs cooked over an open fire on shore while we watched for flags. We caught a fair amount of pickerel and yellow perch, leaving them on the ice for the hawks and two eagles that soared overhead waiting for such a meal.

On Sunday, I was busy with chores once again, and then the entire brood of us Littlefields enjoyed a huge meal at my grandparents. Incredible food, great stories from the Uncs and Pup, and much laughter and fun with the cousins. Who had time to think about some stupid story?

Then, inevitably, it was Monday. I walked into fourth period English and immediately noticed an ever-growing stack of papers on Miss Farley's desk as each of my classmates dutifully submitted their stories to her. I ducked my head and was hopeful that no one would notice that I went directly to my desk. It may have been the quietest I'd ever been in class.

Ol' "eagle-eye" Farley noticed.

I admitted that I hadn't written a solitary word for my story as yet. I was more than a little ashamed, and I figured I was going to pay the price for my procrastination.

I was right.

Miss Farley said, "You will not join the class while we go over these stories. You will not participate in recess. You will go to the principal's office and write your story. If it is not finished by the end of class, you will not participate in any other recess today in your other classes. You will return to the principal's office to work on the story. If your story is not complete by the end of school today, you will stay after school, with me, in the auditorium, and work on it until it is finished. Do you understand?"

I hung my head and nodded. I grabbed my books and legal pad, and made the long painful trip to the principal's office with Miss Farley herding me. She explained the situation to the school's secretary sitting in the front room of the principal's office. The principal came out, gave me the evil eye and pointed to a desk in the corner I supposed was there explicitly for me, and returned to his office. I sat at the desk and pondered what my story should be.

I was able to write and complete the story before the end of the school day, but there were no recesses or lunch for me that day. Miss Farley accepted my scribbling at the end of the day, looked at me with disappointment, and remarked, "It's highly likely that you will not receive a passing grade, Mitch."

I nodded my understanding, profusely apologized and promised this would never happen again.

She let me off the hook with a dismissive shake of her head, and I joined the line of kids outside waiting for the bus to take us home. No one said anything to me. I felt as though I had become a leper of sorts. Probably the other kids didn't really give two hoots, but they could sense I was not in the greatest of moods, so they left me alone.

The next day at school, when I went to fourth period, Miss Farley took me outside the classroom and began to ask me some questions.

"Mitch, did you copy the story you submitted to me?"

I looked at her puzzled, "What do you mean?"

She said, "Did you read a story and then copy it for your story?"

I assured her this was not the case. I told her I just started writing the story because it was the first thing that popped into my head, and it sort of took on a life of its own as I wrote it. I said, "Miss Farley, there are no books with a story like that in the principal's office. I am telling you the truth."

She said, "Mitch, this story is very good. You wrote this story in about two hours altogether. I am impressed. But, as you did not do as you were asked or expected to do, I cannot give you the grade I feel it deserves. I will pass you with a C-, because it is that good, and I expect you to be more attentive in the future. You should learn from this. You should write more stories. You seem to have a knack for it."

This is where I should tell you that I was shocked, and relieved, but it wouldn't be true. Somehow I knew. I knew when I was writing that story, lost in it, letting it take a life of its own as it developed, that it was pretty good. It dawned on me that perhaps I did have a knack for storytelling.

Miss Farley decided it was good enough to have me read the story at the next school assembly. In front of the entire school. Ugh. My first crack at public speaking. Or maybe it was her way at paying me back for not following the rules. I don't know. Reading the story in front of the entire school was hand-trembling, nervous-beyond-compare, excruciating, but creating a story that others liked to read was euphoric. I was hooked. I've been writing stories ever since, and I bless Miss Farley every time I write another story.

So, this one is for Miss Farley. I'll never forget you, or how you nurtured this hyper-active kid by encouraging me to write my stories and to get lost in them.

The following story is a re-creation of that story. Keep in mind, I wrote this story as an eleven year old, 46 years ago, and this IS a re-creation. My writing skills and vocabulary have hopefully developed a tad since then, but I have tried to tell the story as close to the original as possible.

The Fox

The boy was asleep. He was dreaming of a summer day, warm and sunny, being spent with his dad and swimming at Randall Pond at the little poly-ethylene covered hut they called a camp. While the boy swam, his father was fishing off the other side of the little peninsula that jutted out in front of the camp.

The father began to holler, "I got one on, Jack. Stay on that side of the peninsula so you don't get caught up in the line."

Just as his father was reeling the fish onto the shore, loud noises reverberated through the boys head, popping the dream bubble, and he came awake with a start. The boy rubbed his eyes as he listened for the source of the noise that woke him up.

It was the chickens squawking. A lower thrum of collective clucking punctuated by high pitched squawks. Something, or somebody, was in the hen house, causing the laying hens to have a fit. He piled out of bed, dressing quickly in the cold, and clattered down over the stairs where he met his grandfather in the kitchen heading towards the shed for his heavy jacket and then to investigate the noise. The boy followed after his grandfather and pulled on his heavy mackinaw and wool stocking hat and mittens as they headed out the shed door and ran to the hen house. The wind was howling, making the tree limbs dance and the recent snow of the last two days' storm lash at their faces. It was midnight, very dark, but the pristine white of the snow illuminated the ground bushes, and the path to the hen house was easy to see.

When they reached the hen house and turned the corner, to the door side of the building, facing away from the farmhouse and towards the woods, some forty feet away, on the other side of the pasture, a bolt of neon orange/red flew out of the coop, dragging a hen in its mouth, leaving a trail of scarlet red blood in the snow.

The grandfather uttered a profanity, then looked down at the boy and said, "That damn fox is going to be back. These hens are an easy meal. We need to figure out how she is getting in." He instructed the boy to run back to the house and grab his large flashlight from the shed and return with it so they could inspect. The boy nodded and scooted back to the warmth of the shed, grabbed his grandfather's flashlight from the shelves on one wall, beside the coat hooks, and went back out into the cold darkness. He didn't turn the light on as he could easily see his grandfather standing there looking off towards the woods, wondering if the fox was still nearby. His grandfather patted a thanks on the boy's shoulder as he took the flashlight and spotlighted the door and wall of the hen house. Playing the beam over the building and the ground in front of it, they noticed the blood trail led underneath the building. The fox had found access through the floor somehow. The grandfather twisted the 6" by 3" piece of pine board that swiveled on a spike nailed into the wall, that acted as a door latch, and entered the hen house. The hens started clucking and squawking again as he played the light over the floor. The floor was covered in feathers and chicken waste, mixed with water and grain spillage, that formed a 6' crust that even in the cold smelled so badly of ammonia that it always made Jack take a deep breath and hold it when he entered the coop. The spotlight showed a hole in the corner of the floor, under the three shelves that acted as roosts, made out of 6" pine boards supported by home-made wooden braces that ran the length of the back wall of the coop. Jack always thought of them as bunk beds for the chickens. The hole was cut to allow the chickens to leave the confines of the coop and strut around outside in the chicken-wire open air pen. The pen was 10' by 15', and the 8' high wire fencing was attached to both ends of the coop, then out to posts driven into the ground every 6'. The grandfather played the light around the coop and determined there was no other way into the coop except the door itself, which had been closed and secured by the wooden slat. He then went outside the coop and played the light along the pen, where he found the spot where the fox had entered, then exited with the hen in her mouth. There, they saw, was a place where the wire fencing had pulled away from where it was attached to the side of the coop near the ground. A hole, more of a flap, of 12", with a trail of blood leading out into the pasture, towards the woods beyond. The grandfather muttered, "We should have paid more attention and fixed this when we gathered eggs."

Jack knew this was his fault. After all, it was he who gathered the eggs every afternoon when he got home from school.

"I'm sorry, Pupa, I wasn't paying attention."

The grandfather kicked snow until it was piled above the open flap of fence, sealing off the hole, and said, "It's not just your fault, Jack, I come feed the hens every morning. I should have noticed, too."

He went on, "I'll fix this in the morning after you go to school, once you and I come back from the woods."

Jack looked at his grandfather. "The woods?" He didn't understand.

The grandfather patted Jack on the shoulder and said, "Let's get in where it's warm and I'll explain."

They trudged to the farmhouse and entered into the shed, removing their jackets, hats and mittens, hanging them on the pegs on the wall next to the shelves. The grandfather set the flashlight on the shelves and opened the door leading into the kitchen. He sat at the kitchen table and beckoned Jack to join him in the chair opposite him. As Jack sat down the grandfather explained, "Jack, that fox has found herself a place to feed, and to feed her young. We must stop that. We cannot have her terrorizing the hens and picking them off one at a time. As it is, it will likely take a week or more for the hens to settle down enough to produce eggs again, and we can't afford to lose any more hens. You understand how important those eggs are to this family, don't you?"

Jacked nodded his head and asked the grandfather, "What are we gonna do in the woods, Pupa?"

"We are going to be up at dawn, and we are going to track that fox in the fresh snow. That blood trail will help, but we must do this at first daylight before the trail is covered by new snow. You should get to bed and get as much rest as you can, I'll call you when it is time to go, and you can take the 30-30 I gave you for Christmas with you."

Jack smiled. He was excited about taking his new gun with him. Except for a little target practice, he hadn't had a chance to use it since he was given the gun as a Christmas present by his grandparents. His grandfather had traded with a neighboring farmer for the gun. The cost was two hens and a ewe from their flock of sheep. It was a stiff price, but his grandfather said it was important that Jack have a gun to hunt with and to help protect the farm animals from vermin. After all he was now 11 years old. It was time for him to learn how to hunt and how to use a gun.

They got up from the table and wished each other a good night. The grandfather walked through the front room, used as the living room, into the downstairs bedroom he shared with Jack's grandmother. Jack crept upstairs to his bedroom, trying to be quiet so as to not wake his mother, sleeping in the other upstairs bedroom. He used the bathroom at the head of the stairs and then went into his room and undressed and climbed under the covers. The bed was cold and it would take a couple of minutes for the blankets to capture his body heat and be warm under the covers. As he lay there warming up and drifting off, he thought of his father.

His father had been called off to war. He was in Vietnam, and Jack and his family waited anxiously every day for the mailman to come to see if there was a letter from him. They would usually receive a letter from his father twice a week, the letters describing how this country he was forced to be in was so very different from Maine. The people were nice, he said, but he had a hard time understanding their language. He was sure looking forward to coming home and being on the farm with his family. Jack missed his father more than he could express, and prayed that he would be home soon, safe and sound, every night before he fell asleep.

Just as Jack was nodding off he started to dream about a fox. The fox was beautiful. Her coat was almost iridescent in different shades of orange and red, with black outlines around her eyes and muzzle, with a snow white tip to her tail. Her liquid brown eyes expressed intelligence and she seemed to be smiling as she easily loped through the foot and a half of snow. Leaping over blow downs and nimbly side stepping tree trunks as she made her way through the forest, she was a magnificent creature.

It seemed only moments had passed when Jack slowly pulled himself out of his dream at the sound of his grandfather beckoning him to get dressed. He opened his eyes to see his grandfather standing over his bed, and sat up. "I'll be right down Pupa."

He scrambled out of bed, used the bathroom quickly, and then dressed for a trip into the woods beyond the pasture. Wearing long johns, wool socks, woolen pants, and a heavy sweater his mother had knitted for him over his flannel shirt, he went down the stairs to the kitchen. His grandfather was sitting in a kitchen chair, oiling both Jack's 30-30, and his own double barreled 12-gauge shotgun. He looked up and asked, "Ready to go, son?"

"Yes sir."

They went out into the shed and geared up with their boots, coats, hats and gloves. His grandfather grabbed a set of binoculars from the cabinet which held the guns and ammo at the far end of the shed. He passed Jack ten 30-30 shells, and then handed him his 30-30. He pocketed ten double ought buckshot 12-gauge shells and grabbed his shot gun, nodded at the door leading outside and said, "Let's go."

As they trudged towards the barn to climb through the fence into the pasture that led to the woods, Jack looked east to see a hint of pink on the horizon, signifying that day was breaking, and he also noticed a multitude of stars still glittering above. It was going to be a clear and sunny day. As he and his grandfather trudged across the pasture, looking for the blood trail of the hen, and the footprints of the fox, his grandfather was talking in a very soft voice, "Jack, we will need to be very quiet. This fresh snow will help us move without noise, and should help us follow the trail easily. When we find the fox's den, hopefully we can catch her when she comes out. When I tell you, I want you to load your gun with five shells, and make sure you keep it on safety until you are ready to shoot. Ok, son?"

"Ok, Pupa," Jack whispered and a shiver of cold and of excitement wiggled up his spine. Jack mimicked his grandfather, moving cautiously, quietly, his eyes shifting back and forth, taking everything in. His ears were straining to hear any noise or movement, his breathing shallow, and he sniffed the air, hoping to catch any scent wafting in the cold dry morning air. Before they reached the other side of the pasture, about 15 yards before the wood line, they found the fox's trail. His grandfather smiled and nodded towards the woods. They walked very slowly, watching for any movement as they climbed through the fence and stepped into the woods.

They followed the trail for another quarter mile as it meandered through the woods, stepping around thickets and trees, ducking under low-hanging branches, and side stepping rocks sticking up out of the snow. His grandfather stopped, leaned into Jack and whispered, "See that outcropping of rocks on that knoll up ahead?" Jack nodded as he looked at the pile of rocks with what appeared to be a hole or entry way inside the pile. His grandfather whispered, "I think that is her den, and my guess is, she may be out hunting this morning, looking for food for her young. If we are lucky, we will catch her coming back. I am going to sneak over to the left and hide among those trees. If she comes from that direction or from the east, I will take her. You hide in this clump of firs and if she comes from this direction, or from the south, you take her. Load your gun, leave it on safety until you are ready to shoot. You will have only one shot at her. Make it count."

Jack nodded his understanding and stepped into a tripod of firs that screened him from view, but allowed him to see the rock pile and see to the south through the semi-dense woods. He loaded the 30-30 with five shots, making sure to click on the safety, and watched while his grandfather sneaked to the north and hid amongst another stand of firs, looking east towards the fox's den. Jack stood perfectly still as he had been taught. He tried to breathe through his nose so to limit the amount of vapor he produced. His eyes intently searched the woods beyond, looking for movement.

It seemed like hours but was probably only ten minutes when THERE!...there was a flash of orange, coming at Jack from the south. Jack held his breath and watched as his heart started to pound in his chest. He was trying not to move a muscle. In another 20 seconds he saw the fox. She was heading at a meandering pace, her nose first to the ground, then her nose would go up into the air, smelling, trying to catch a scent on the slight wind blowing towards the north, which served to cover their scents. She seemed to be wary, but unaware of Jack and his grandfather. He knew his grandfather was watching the fox too, but the fox was coming from the south, meaning it was Jack's shot. The fox kept coming and now was within 30 yards of Jack. He slowly raised the rifle to his shoulder, carefully, soundlessly, clicking off the safety, and sited the fox down the barrel using just the tip of the metal site at the end of the barrel. The fox stopped, holding one front paw off the ground as she looked to the east inquisitively.

She was as beautiful as the fox in his dreams.

His grandfather's words were hammering in his mind's ear, "You will have only one shot at her. Make it count."

Jack took a slow breath and held it. Slowly and steadily he squeezed the trigger. The gun roared and bucked against his shoulder. The fox dropped in her tracks, kicked once and lay still. Jack's shot was true.

He took a long shaky breath, and clicked the gun's safety back on as he lowered it. Stepping out of the stand of firs, he started walking to the fox. He saw his grandfather coming from the north, walking to meet him where the fox lay in the snow, a scarlet red stain in the snow near her neck. Then, they were standing over the fox, looking down at her. Jack turned away from his grandfather so he wouldn't see the tears running down

Jack's cheeks. His grandfather put his arm around the boy, led him to a blow down, brushed the snow away, leaned his and Jack's guns against the tree, and sat down beside him. Jack snuffled, wiped his face and said to his grandfather, "What a damn baby huh Pupa?"

"No, Jack. You just did what a man has to do. Like your Daddy over there in 'Nam, sometimes we have to do things we don't want to do for the good of the family."

Jack nodded, "Yeah, I guess so. Can I bury her, Pupa? She was so beautiful, she deserves that from me."

His grandfather pulled the boy a little tighter to him, "You know Jack, she was beautiful, that pelt will bring at least $35. That's money this family could use, but you shot her, it's your decision."

The grandfather stood, and said, "I'm gonna take the guns and head back to the house. I'll leave you here to decide what you're gonna do. Don't take too long, Jack. You shouldn't miss school."

Jack waited ten minutes until his grandfather had crossed over the fence and was almost across the pasture, when he stood up and tied the length of bailing twine he had in his coat pocket around the neck of the fox and began the journey back to the barn, where the fox would need to be skinned out and her pelt would be nailed and stretched to the barn wall to dry. His grandfather was right, the family could use the money, and his father was doing his duty over there in Vietnam, Jack needed to do his duty, too.

When he got back to the barn, his grandfather was milking one of the four milking cows the family had, and told Jack, "Tell ya what Jack, it's already past 6:30, and your school bus will be picking you up in less than 45 minutes. You don't have much time to get ready. I'll skin out that fox for you today, and you can help me stretch out the pelt after school, OK?"

All day at school Jack couldn't get the fox off his mind. He didn't feel any pride in what he had done, but he did realize why it was necessary. He was glad when the final bell rang and he was able to escape to the school bus for the ride home. When he got off the bus, he went past the shed door, directly to the barn, where he found his grandfather had skinned out the fox and disposed of the body. He was waiting for Jack to help nail and stretch the hide to the barn wall so it could dry properly. He said, "Jack, you need to change out of your school clothes before we do this. If you don't, your mother and grandmother will be tanning both our hides."

Jack smiled. He knew that was true. So, he climbed the steps into the shed and stepped inside. As he was taking off his coat he heard a whimper. Puzzled, he looked around until he found the source of the noise. In a cardboard box, against the back wall of the shed, was a little red furry creature that he was delighted to discover to be an Irish Setter puppy. His heart soared as he picked the pup up, noticing that it was a boy, and nuzzled it. The pup was nipping at his nose and lapping him over and over as he squirmed and wiggled in Jack's arms. The pup could not be more than eight weeks old he was so little. Jack was thrilled. His grandfather somehow appeared behind him and asked, "What you gonna name your dog, son?" Jack looked at his grandfather with a smile from ear to ear and responded with one word. "Fox."

About the Author

I was born into a large family in the mid 1950s, in Belfast, Maine. My family owned and operated three working farms during my childhood, and the entire family worked these farms. It is these formative years, this family, those farms, and that way of life that is the background for the short stories in *Memories of Shucking Peas*. After high school, I moved from the farm and have tried my hand at many things, ranging from working in the chicken factories in Belfast to becoming a licensed stock broker—along with multiple other incarnations. With this "jack of all trades, master of none" approach, I've experienced many different perspectives in life and each of them has its own story to be told.

Storytelling is an art form that is fading away with each generation and one that I cherish from my own childhood years when my elders would spin yarns that never grew old to my ears and always stimulated my over-active imagination. It has become my mission in life to be that storyteller of my generation.

Being a 16th generation Mainer, I'm told, makes me a qualified native. Even though I've traded in the bib overalls of the farm and now live in the "big city" of Bangor, I cherish my farm boy roots, and will always live in my beloved Maine. I am blessed to still have that large and loving family, most who continue to live and work nearby the farms I grew up on, which includes my three adult children, and at present count, three grandchildren, who I unashamedly spoil horribly.

CPSIA information can be obtained
at www.ICGtesting.com
Printed in the USA
FFOW05n1617280415

9 780945 980681